# Psychoanalysis and Mythology

BY

KARL JOHAN KARLSON

A DISSERTATION SUBMITTED TO THE FACULTY OF CLARK UNIVERSITY, WORCESTER, MASS., IN PARTIAL FULFILMENT OF THE REQUIREMENTS FOR THE DEGREE OF DOCTOR OF PHILOSOPHY, AND ACCEPTED ON THE RECOMMENDATION OF G. STANLEY HALL

Reprinted from the JOURNAL OF RELIGIOUS PSYCHOLOGY
November, 1914, Vol. VII, pp. 137-213

# PSYCHOANALYSIS AND MYTHOLOGY*

By KARL JOHAN KARLSON,
*Fellow in Psychology, Clark University*

CONTENTS



## I. Introductory

In recent years particular interest in myths and mythmaking has been aroused by Anthropology, Social Psychology, as well

* The writer wishes to express his gratitude to President G. Stanley Hall, Ph. D., LL. D., and Professors Alexander F. Chamberlain, Ph. D., and William H. Burnham, Ph. D., of Clark University for their very helpful suggestions and kind criticism in the preparation of this paper.

as by the Freudian school. Boas and Ehrenreich have paid special attention to the problem. Wundt has devoted a great deal of energy and time to expound the *Völker-Psychologie*. And the Freudian school has busied itself with a certain phase of the problem. Everybody seems to have begun to look at primitive man and his culture in a quite different way from what was formerly the custom. All this has caused modern man to consider his ancestors more sympathetically and regard primitive man with all his faults and defects really human. This paper is a preliminary study and purposes to treat the mental products of primitive man, and "near" primitive man, from a psychological point of view, in order to discover what mental processes were involved in the formation of the myth as well as folklore in general.

## 1. *Definition of Myths.*

First of all let us ask: What is a myth? Gennep (26) says that it is a legend localized in time and space outside human reach but within that of divine personages. A legend he defines as being a story in which "the place is indicated with precision and the personages some determined individuals whose acts have a foundation which seems historic and heroic." And "one can understand by myth a legend in relation to the supernatural world and explain it indeed from the rites." In this respect he differs radically from Brinton (11) who maintains that no myth ever rose from the rite, but that the rite always arose from the myth, whether we are able to explain it or not; the old myth which gave rise to the rite, may be lost. Boas (9) on the other hand believes "that the tale as such is older than its mythological significance."

John Fiske (23) undoubtedly tries to bring in and apply the generic or evolutionary idea into mythology for he defines a myth as

"In its origin an explanation, by the uncivilized mind, of some natural phenomena, not an allegory, not an esoteric symbol,—for the ingenuity is wasted which strives to detect in myths the remnants of a refined primeval science,—but an explanation."

Tylor (79) maintains that

"myth is sham history, the fictitious narrative of events that never happened."

Ruskin (67a) remarks:

"A myth, in its simplest definition, is a story with a meaning attached to it other than that which it seems to have at first, and the *fact* that it has such a meaning is generally marked by some of its circumstances being extraordinary."

Ruskin seems to be radically at variance with John Fiske who maintained that a myth *was* an explanation and he that it *needs* one.

Max Müller (54) holds that

"mythology which was the bane of the ancient world, is, in truth, a disease of language." "The origin of mythological phraseology is always the same; it is language forgetting herself." "It is in fact the dark shadow which language throws on thought and which never disappears till language becomes commensurate with thought which it never will." "Mythology in the highest sense is the power exerted by language upon thought in every possible sphere of mental activity, and I do not hesitate to call the whole history of philosophy, from Thales down to Hegel, an uninterrupted battle against mythology, a constant protest of thought against language."

I have given this rather lengthy quotation from Max Müller to show his trend of thought. He has had perhaps more to do with the "Sacred Books of the East" than any other Westerner and thus has had a good opportunity to form his opinion about their subject-matter. But it is strange how mind can lose itself in the narrow paths of thought unguided by any psychological insight.

Forlong (24) regards myths as

"history which we have not yet been able to read." "Zeuses and Ios, Europas and Helenas, Titans and Toths and gods are all history in the process of incubation; we must unravel the skein and see the real actors, their acts, principles and faiths."

Abraham (1) says that

"myth is a piece of overcome infantile mental life of a people. It contains (in a curtailed form) the infantile wish of a people."

In regard to the origin of the myths Wundt (88) writes that

"the last source of all myth formation, of all religious feelings and ideas is the individual fantasy-activity; even those structures which have been developed under the condition of communal life possess entirely the character of a creation of fancy. In myth the folk-fantasy connects the event with reality. In religion it creates from the contents of these events its ideas concerning the cause and purpose of the human existence."

Definitions could be multiplied but the above cited may be

enough to show what divergence of opinions exists among those who have studied this subject. Interesting to be sure they are, for they show what other persons have thought about the myths and also reflect the special interest by which they were guided. In Max Müller's definition the philologist appears plainly, in John Fiske's the historian and so on.

The Greek word *mythos,* which has been transplanted into almost every language, means simply "a word" or "a saying," and the definitions that make myths history which we are not yet able to read coincide fairly well with this. Myth is then a word, a saying, an expression by primitive man of his thoughts and ideas about himself and the world in which he lives. As John Fiske (23) says: "They are the earliest recorded utterances of men concerning the visible phenomena of the world into which they were born." Myth is thus history, obscured to be sure by the many transformations which everything human has to go through from time to time, but history, nevertheless, recording what primitive man thought and felt in the first stages of his existence as man, be it either as a race or as an individual.

### 2. *Myth and Language*

Max Müller's degeneration theory, as Wundt (88) calls it, could never be wholly true, if at all. Bacon's theory, later taken up by Gladstone and others, that the myths are glimpses of an old civilization, is not worth considering except in so far as it has any bearing on Max Müller's. But to build up a system entirely on the remnants of the names of the gods by tracing them back from one language to another is not far from nonsense. Who knows whether the original language, if such there be, is still in existence, dead or alive, for language can exist though dead? The further back one goes the greater do the gapes become in the mythological ideas which finally disappear completely. Moreover, it can not be concluded from this procedure that the ideas are simpler and purer the further back one goes, nor that conformity of names means the same thing in different languages and at different periods, since the mythological ideas as well as all other ideas are dependent upon both subjective and objective conditions which constantly change as well as being subject to changes themselves.

But even if languages were stable, fixed, *i. e.*, did not change in any respect during endless times; even if words spelled the same way everywhere and always and had the same meaning among all nations at all times; and even if the ideas conveyed by the words and the sentences all the time and everywhere were the same, we should nevertheless have myths to explain and mythological ideas to expound and elucidate, because, as Schleiermacher (39) said, there is a deeper common principle underlying it all which must be taken into consideration, and that we must always reason from what the religious consciousness *says* to what it *means*. And if this is true of the religious consciousness, it is also true of consciousness in general.

But now since language is not stable, either, but undergoes changes together with the human race, so that a word may utterly lose its original meaning and take on a wholly different one even in the same language, not to speak of the meaning of the same word in different languages, the case is even more complicated. Thus, in order to find the right meaning of the words and be able to read the history of primitive man and see what he thought, believed, worshipped and feared, and at the same time find out his mental ability and procedure, it is not only necessary to inversely unfold the changes which the languages have gone through in their development but also to unravel the mysteries of the soul and see what he really thought and felt. By these means a fair accuracy may be reached.

That words will change meaning when passing from one language to another is too well known to be reiterated, but an illustration of Max Müller's procedure and conclusion may be given by referring to his and his followers' explanation of Zeus and the Trojan war, remembering, however, that some of the etymologies have been seriously attacked by Mahaffy (52). In the Greek a large number of names, especially of the gods and heroes, have no meaning, but if traced back to Sanskrit a meaning may be found in them. Thus Zeus or Jupiter is Dyaus pitar and means in the Veda "sky" and Hermes or Sarameias "the breeze of the summer morning." Athene or Ahana means "the light of daybreak," which causes John Fiske to write: "Thus we are enabled to understand why the Greeks described her as sprung from the forehead of Zeus." Helena or Sarama means "the fickle twilight," whom the Panis, or nightdemons, the prototype of the Hellenic Paris, strive to seduce from her allegiance to the solar monarch. In Greek all these meanings were lost and their origin completely forgotten. In the Vedas the Trojan war was carried on in the sky between the bright deities and the nightdemons, but in Greek it was located on the shores of the Hellespont, perhaps on account of some historical event that might have happened there. A later development of the Trojan war is to be sure plain from the great difference in the characters of those taking part.

Kuhn (49) and after him Abraham (1) have tried to show the very same thing in regard to the Prometheus myth, tracing it back to the Hindu Pramantha which has a wholly different meaning from the Greek derivative Prometheus. When the origin of the word was lost, the original meaning was also lost and a new attached to the new word, to fit the new environment and the new thought. But this changing of words and with them a new meaning and a new explanation must have been a slow process and taken place unconsciously, especially if Boas is right, who maintains that language arose unconsciously and was unconsciously applied to the objects in which the people had special interest.

### 3. *Divisions of Myths*

The theory that myth is an explanation by primitive man of the objects, events and happenings around him does not contain the whole truth. This theory applies directly only to the so-called nature myths which treat of the natural objects and phenomena surrounding man in his primeval habitat. These myths which apparently are the oldest and to be understood simply as explanations, ought to be divided into two groups: those that deal with the natural objects proper, and those that deal with the natural phenomena. To be sure these are not clearly divided and often overlap one another. There is no symbolism in them, at least not at first. The sun was the sun and nothing else, a living being, either the greatest god, a god among the gods, a messenger of the god, or an attribute of a god, carried over the heavens. The same is true of most if not all the natural objects and phenomena.

In course of time there grew up another kind of myths which has been more troublesome than the nature myths: the so-called

Hero myths or, as they ought to be designated, Social myths or Culture myths. These originated in a wholly different way and for a wholly different purpose, although they contain a sort of explanation, too, but not in the same sense as the nature myths. The social myths are the outgrowth of man's feelings and emotions stored away down in the deep recesses of the human psyche and for whose expression a totally different mental procedure must be resorted to. The nature myths have primitive science that is reasoning as their foundation; the social myths have feelings and emotions as their foundation. They have therefore taken wholly different paths in their further development. The nature myths have developed into sciences of all kinds and descriptions, while the social myths have developed into poetry, art, religion, ethics, aesthetics, etc. Both of them blend and overlap here and there, because it is impossible to keep two streams of thought that originate in the same or identical psyche and led by the same human hands entirely free from intermixture, even if one be purer than the other, and the natural sciences contain less of feelings and emotions than the normative and literary, and the normative and literary sciences contain less of cold reason and scientific accuracy than the natural. But both are generically human.

Symbolism is closely connected with myths. One kind of it arose when the gods began to be separated from the natural objects, hewn out of them, so to speak, and the Greeks got their Zeus, and the Scandinavians their Odin, etc., with all the gods and goddesses who no longer dwelt among them but had to be represented in some way. Another kind arose when some affections were to be presented and could not be so in their real nature, owing to the fact that society had fixed a certain custom which prescribed the procedure approved of in a given instance. These two, a mental and a social phenomena, are responsible for all symbolism that has later developed.

Thus, when the significance or right meaning of an object or a phenomenon begins to become conscious, it begins also to lose its anthropomorphic character, and in the transitory stage which begins symbolism appears and takes the place of anthropomorphization of the inorganic world. Animals and other objects become symbols of the powers in nature and worshipped and revered as representatives of these powers. But as man rises in his mental ability and activity, for function precedes, his gods become more and more abstract until there is hardly anything more left than the mere thought in Bostrom's sense. The symbols continue to be used even in this period, and it is a question whether they will ever be wholly discarded.

### 4. *Myth and Poetry*

The relationship between myth and poetry and literary fiction is in reality very close, closer even than one at first is ready to admit. But that their general features are more alike than different is seen at a hasty glance. Indeed, the poet still lives, moves, and has his being in the myth-making age. Says Tylor (79):

"Poetry has so far kept alive in our minds the old animative theory of nature, that it is no great effort to us to fancy the water-spout a huge giant or a sea-monster, and to depict in what we call appropriate metaphor its march across the fields of ocean."

And Quantz (62) maintains that

"the poets have never lost sight of the thought that man is only an essential part of the great unity of nature, and to them the trees, the flowers, and the streams have ever been living things of thought and feeling, desire and will."

Zeller (89) places poetry, mythology and religion on the same level and holds that we get them all from such sources as the feelings which arise in our consciousness when we in the spring morning take a walk in the country, by the sea, under the stars, from such instinctive needs as we feel in the thunderstorms, floods, battles, famines, or sickness and from the experience of common family and social life, and that they interpret these needs and feelings and preserve a faithful record of the wishes, fears and hopes of the prehistoric people; indeed the poets are the old theologians. And Wundt (88) says that

"the myth-forming and the poetic imaginations do not differ in their inner essence but only from their external and internal conditions to which they are subjected at a given time and within a given community."

Poetry is not a voluntary invention and myth an involuntary or unconscious product of the soul but both are the result of the same mental activities and belong to the same sphere. So fundamental factors of mental life as will and consciousness can not possibly be lacking in mythological thought and present in poetry. They are either lacking in both or present in both.

To be sure poetry may be on a higher level than many of the loosely connected myths, but even these have a purpose and an association of ideas, since they connect external phenomena with the wishes, hopes, and fears of the people. The teleological factor is not originally contained in poetry as is seen by the impossibility to distinguish between poetry and myth in many cases.

What we generally call poetry has more of a personal character than the myths, but this difference disappears gradually the more one approaches the real poetry and is entirely lost in the epics or folk-poetry which have perhaps been built up during long ages. The folksoul has here asserted itself, expressed itself, and taken possession of the material through some individuals who are totally lost to the world, perhaps because they so skillfully pluck the strings of the human soul-harp that the tunes became so melodious and intense that they themselves were forgotten. The same is the case in myth; there is indeed no difference between the folk-poetry and the myth. "It is myth," says Wundt. The individual character that may linger with some of them is of a secondary sort; the folk-soul that is laid down in them is the primary. This union between myth, folklore, and folk-soul must have deep psychic roots, penetrating down into the recesses of the soul and from there afford an outlet for the hidden psychic powers and emotions that rule supreme in the human being, otherwise they could not have so much in common, as they really have. If this were not the case, they could not exert such a tremendous influence upon mankind as now is the case. There really seems to have been and still is a psychic need or call for this kind of literary production, a hunger so strong that ages of reflection have not been able to obliterate or even satisfy it.

Furthermore, that the psychic factors which produce poetry also produce myth is seen in the fact that poetry never changes the general feature of the myth, and yet it often takes its raw material and clothes it in a rich and beautiful garb and presents it to the world thus transformed. Indeed poetry begins here. The many versions of the various folk-tales depend upon the environmental conditions and upon the personal equation of the several authors. In substance and in purpose they are all the same. The poetic working over of the raw material makes the myths richer and fuller in content. One completes the other. Thus the poetic expression and form of the Eddas, the Niebelungen Lied, the Kalevala, not to speak of the Iliad and the Odyssey, makes them much more attractive and immortal than were the bare mythological records which underlie these beautiful and aesthetic poems alone presented.

Association of ideas and general experience play a great rôle in the formation and development of myths, but says Wundt (88)

"as long as the association of mythological ideas remains connected with the phenomena which form their substrate the mythformation keeps the character of pure myth, not yet essentially changed by individual, poetic additions, even if they are interwoven with many associations."

To be sure the individual imagination sometimes individualizes the mythic pictures and transforms them from being general into individual, concrete experiences taken place at a certain time and place. The old general ideation, clothed in a poetic garb, becomes very concrete and individual. The characters of Niebelungen Lied are very corporeal and realistic, almost human in their behavior, and perform their deeds at definite places in a generically human way. But when the individual poetic addition becomes too prominent, then the myth loses its special character and the formation becomes poetry pure and simple, but having lost its character of folk-poetry it is soon lost for the world and generations to come will not know very much about it.

## II. Primitive Man and His Mind

### 1. *Development of Man*

Wachter (84) remarks: "Der Mensh ist geworden und nicht erschaffen" and even if DeVries' theory of mutation be true, and man sprang into existence as man with a sudden leap, this "geworden" must of necessity have been a very slow process and ages passed through before he found himself and awoke consciously as man. It makes quite a difference in regard to his mental attitude toward and grasp of the external world whether his becoming man was a slow process or happened with a sudden leap, for in the former case he was gradually being acquainted with and accustomed to the world around him while in the latter he was placed in his position unexpectedly and so rather unaccustomed to it. His relation to the w behind him would also be quite different if he suddenly be man, for in this respect he would be more cut off from ancestral world and his inheritance of what had passed b him be diminished if not altogether nullified. Therefo order to save man from being disinherited we must assume his becoming was a slow process with perhaps small sc leaps here and there in his mental and physical maket the flicker of a burning light that has just been lighted it reaches its full capacity. In this case his mentality w be stored up during ages that passed before him layer by for him to use in his new position.

A sudden leap into prominence, so to speak, would also produced in him a wholly different reaction and mental att toward the world around him. The effect of this might been lasting and detrimental to his further development when an impression or idea enters mind they leave traces them. This is true the more so the lower man stands o upward plane of mental evolution, because the lower he s the less there is in his mind and experience to counterba the impressions and ideas that force themselves upon Just as in early life impressions received remain fixed i mind and may cause great disturbances in the mental act while impressions received later on, when there is a better tation and a more perfect understanding, may not have disturbing effect at all, although they may not be entirely

Thus man's becoming man might not have been so sudden after all, and his orientation might have been some gradual. In this case the magnificence of the phenomena a him slowly became conscious to him, *i. e.*, had some me to him. Then, he strengthened the external impressio inward meditation and thought, warmed by the wonde grandeur of a distant spectacle, such as a thunderstorm, a evening after sunset, when the streaks of lightning illumi the dark firmament as they passed from one cloud to an

Primitive man must necessarily have been strongly emot because there was very little in his experience to counterba and keep in check, when stirred up, the feelings and em which are at the bottom of every human soul, although,

them if occasion demanded it. And the ability to repress the feelings and emotions must have been an important factor in evolution, for only those who could master themselves in strange and trying circumstances would have any chance of survival in the struggle for existence which has always been waged.

### 2. *The One-pair Origin Theory.*

The question of the unity of the human races as they exist to-day may be looked at from two different points of view: The unity of descent and the unity of development. The former has to do with the single pair origin of mankind and the second with the developments along similar lines and according to similar laws. These are two quite different problems and must be settled in quite different ways, and still they amount to the very same thing.

Boas (9) maintains that this question was settled by the thoroughgoing inquiries made into this subject by Waitz (85) who asserts

"that the question of the unity of the species and the nature of man especially belongs to those branches of knowledge which treat of the intellect,"

so that whether there are any physical differences or not does not belong to the subject. The notion that there must be a dominant white race which shall be served by all others and which may treat them as it sees fit he repudiates strongly. Agassiz (85) maintained that there were as many original types of man as there are typically different peoples on earth. He based his conclusions on analogies drawn from bees and other social animals and wanted to show that the descent from one pair was highly improbable; but it is difficult to see how this analogy could be carried out in all cases.

The attempt that has been made to show that descent from one pair is preferable, since it is not advisable to multiply causes and one miracle is more acceptable than many, Waitz meets by the assertion that

"it is clear that a multiplication of agents is something different from a great complication of acting causes and that as regards miracles science can not concern itself about the degree of admissibility but about the suspension of the natural laws which are in conflict with science, for a mir

He also maintained that the "probably unsolvable problem of descent from one pair or several pairs" is of minor importance. To be sure, the positive proofs of descent from one pair are very scanty and the theory is very improbable, since nature would not in this case perhaps more than in any other hang the existence and preservation of a species on so slender a thread as a single pair. Nature works always toward an end and it knows of no parsimony in obtaining it. The developmental factors which caused one pair to spring into existence must have been the same everywhere, if the environment and circumstances were the same, and these could not have changed so quickly and so radically in the same place so as to preclude the production of any more pairs, and if they did, this pair, just produced, would not have been able to survive or produce offspring that would have been able to survive. Thus, it is difficult to see why just one pair should have been developed in one place and no more. It is, however, easy to see that environment might have been, and in all probability was, more favorable in one region than in another. But, according to Weisman, environment does not play any great rôle in bringing about changes, either in the individual or in the species. If we thus have to rule out environment, too, the problem becomes even more difficult, because environment has always been the dumping ground for our ignorance, for we have there deposited what we have been unable to explain otherwise. DeVries' theory of mutation would possibly help us some, but the conclusion would necessarily be that, when nature had produced one pair of homo sapiens, it could do no more, for it took all its human-making strength and energy to produce this one pair.

The objection might be raised that, if there were more than one pair, how can the human race be one, but this objection may be met simply by saying that in producing man nature produced a certain species according to well established laws and nothing could get into this hierarchy or be recognised as belonging to it which had not the essential qualifications. It is thus not necessary to assume, as Agassiz did, as many original types of man as there are typically different peoples to-day, even if we assume that more than one pair sprang into existence at one or several places [illegible] takes place between races will ultimately change the original types that interchange and produce a new type perhaps wholly different from either of the original, depending upon the dominant characteristics and the circumstances under which the intermixture takes place.

Thus, whether we assume the origin of one single pair or several the result will be the same. In either case we must also assume a considerable degree of mutability of the type as well as intermixture, although we do not know whether intermixture has taken place at all in some cases and how far it has progressed in others.

Consequently, whether man has developed slowly or come into existence with a sudden leap; whether he is monogenous or polygenous does not make so much difference, for the moment he was pronounced *man*, he was forever separated from his progenitors as far as the type is concerned and endowed with all the mental and physical attributes and possessions which belong to him as man. He may change physically and mentally and develop along somewhat different lines according to the circumstances under which he lives, but he will always remain fundamentally the same as long as he remains man.

### 3. *The Oneness of Human Mind*

That no two races are exactly alike in physical or mental development and characteristics is a too well-known fact to be reiterated. If all were alike we should not have different races. And still the assertion is made and maintained that man is fundamentally one, and that this unity depends more on intellectual ability than physical development. To be sure one race may be foremost in one kind of human activity and another in another, but seldom is anyone behind in all. And Boas (9) says: "The weight of evidence is on the whole in favor of an essential similarity of mental development in the different races with the probability of variations in the type of mental characteristics." Heredity and environment may of course cause different people to react differently to the same stimuli, but where these are the same and the stimuli not strongly different the same reaction will take place from similar stimuli. These tw[illegible] experience, play a great rôle in the development of mind, especially how and in what direction it shall develop. They present also two different problems. Says Boas:

"It may be that the minds of different races show differences of organization; that is to say, the laws of mental activity may not be the same for all minds. But it may also be that the organization of mind is practically identical among all races of men, but that its manifestations depend upon the character of the individual experience that is subjected to the action of these laws."

Thus a man may run away when he hears a dog bark, because he has been bitten by a dog, or he may rejoice, because he is lost and now expects to find someone, or else he may take it as the first greeting from his home which he is nearing. The differences in these mental manifestations surely depend upon the individual experience and not upon the mental organization as such.

Experimental psychology has taught us that man is thinking and acting according to definite laws and that these laws are frightfully rigid. Mind seems to work like a machine: Given the same material and it will infallibly grind out the same result, all things being equal. Post (10) was so struck by this fact that he said: "We do not think; thinking merely goes on within us." Maybe it is not so simple as that but there is nevertheless some truth in it. Psychology has also taught us that ideas originate from impressions on the sensory nerves by association according to definite laws.

Brinton (10) calls this the most startling discovery in recent times.

But if man's mind developed in practically the same way and according to the same laws everywhere, and if consequently the organization of mind is the same in all races, the differences, which exist between the races, in mental development are of degree and not of kind. The question remains open, however, according to Boas (9) which "characteristics of primitive man are causes of his low culture and which are caused by it." Abstract thought *e. g.* occurs only in a comparatively high stage of mental development and is said certainly not to exist in children and primitive men. These are bound down to concrete objects and handle them as if they were flesh of their flesh and bones [illegible] properties as they are themselves. The external world is a part of themselves or at least made up of the same elements as they are and as such they treat it. The dividing line between the animate and inanimate world is not clear, and the distinction between animals and man is not sharply drawn. The abstractness, the condition, and the attribute of the object are not comprehended and therefore must be expressed in concrete forms. Sickness and health are regarded as independent realities which can be taken out and put into the body as the case might require. The child has still to go through the same stage of development and the adult is not quite free from it. But whether this condition is a necessary one or brought about by circumstances are two different questions. That there was a time when abstract thought was impossible may be quite certain but whether this can be prolonged by environment is another thing. It certainly seems so, for Boas found that the Indians were capable of abstract thought whenever there was any occasion for it and could very readily learn to use it, but that it was needless in that kind of society in which they live. This is quite natural for when grammatical constructions began to develop and have some meaning, abstract thought began also to develop and enable man to carry on his reasoning and form his concepts about the world in which he is a member.

Concepts and distinct types of association must have originated unconsciously, as it oftentimes still does, in the customs and habits which primitive man was gradually forming during his early existence. If these were ever to become conscious it must happen by incidentally or accidentally breaking them off, which occurs as soon and as often as a new factor enters into experience and demands recognition. When this takes place he wakes up to the fact that there is a large content in his mind for which he can give no adequate account except that it is there. Man has always acted more or less customarily and not always for any conscious motive, but primitive man seldom stopped there but proceeded to explain his own acts or desires. But

"the desire to understand one's own actions (as soon as they become conscious) and to get a clear insight into the secrets of the world, manifest [illegible] ...rising that man in all stages of culture begins to speculate on the motives of his own actions,''

says Boas. And again, this

''secondary explanation has nothing to do with the historical origin, but is based upon the general knowledge possessed by the people.''

Therefore, the explanation of the same phenomena may be quite different among different peoples depending upon the knowledge of those that make the explanation. Thus when he was confronted by a particular cosmic event or phenomenon he ransacked his whole mental storehouse to find something that fitted the occasion and gave an explanation of the same satisfactory to his mind. He applied his individual and social life as he saw it to the natural and cosmic events and interpreted them in this way. Thus did the nature myths arise.

The existence of the same myth, or at least of a similar myth, in various parts of the world presents another phase of this problem. The general theory has been and is still held in certain quarters that these myths had a central origin and then spread to or were borrowed by the different peoples who now possess them. Bastian (5) held that they were due to elementary ideas and so inexplicable. Others (Weule, Graebner) believed that they have their origin in the time when mankind was still one before any dispersion had taken place. And still others (Ritter, Guyot, Ratzel) thought that they were caused by the influence of geographical environment upon the life of man. Let us give one example of these myths, the legend of Wilhelm Tell. Fiske (23) has shown that it existed not only in Switzerland where it has been especially immortalized but also in Denmark, Norway, England, Iceland, Finland, Russia, Persia, and supposedly also in India. Dasent (17) observes that it is common to the Turks and Mongolians,

''and a legend of the wild Samojeds, who never heard of Tell or saw a book in their lives, relates it, chapter and verse, of one of their marksmen.''

And John Fiske remarks:

''In all these stories names and motives of course differ; but all contain the same essential incident. It is always an unerring archer who, at the capricious command of a tyrant, shoots from the head of some one dear to him a small object, be it an apple, a nut, or a piece of coin. The archer always provides himself with a second arrow and, when questioned as to the use he intended to make of this extra weapon, the invariable reply is· To kill thee, tyrant, had I slain my son.''

Dasent thinks

''that the story of this bold mastershot was primeval among many tribes and races and that it only crystalized itself around the great name of Tell by that process of attraction which invariably leads a grateful people to throw such mythic wreaths, such garlands of bold deeds of precious memory around the brow of its darling champion.''

And John Fiske thinks

''that when a marvelous occurrence is said to have happened everywhere, we may feel sure that it never happened anywhere. Popular fancies propagate themselves indefinitely, but historical events, especially the striking and dramatic ones, are rarely repeated. The facts here collected lead inevitably to the conclusion that the Tell myth was known, in its general features, to our Aryan ancestors, before they ever left their primitive dwelling-place in central Asia.''

Stories like that of Tell may be multiplied many times and all show that they existed in places simultaneously with such differences as were absolutely necessary in order to fit the particular place and people. But whether they all originated among one people and then spread to others, or grew up independently in various places is not so easily settled. The philologists and historical mythologists as well as some anthropologists favor necessarily a central origin. It can certainly not be denied that there exists a large amount of material that seems to favor such a theory, as for instance the foreign words in the story and the possibility of tracing them back to their origin. But in that case all Aryan languages can be traced back to their supposed mother tongue, more or less. To be sure some of the stories themselves can be traced back to other people and races, from whom they have thus been transmitted as a whole or in part.

But with the Asiatic cradle of the Aryan race still more disputed to-day than it ever was, as is shown by Taylor (78), Much (53), Richards (66) and others, it seems foolish to try to seek the origin of all our myths in Asia. Some of them may have originated there, for, as Petrie (59) has shown, the civilization and culture of southern and southeastern Asia seem undoubtedly to have developed earlier than those of any other region and so presuppose an earlier development of the people living there, owing to more favorable circumstances. But this does not mean that all our myths originated there. Leaving, therefore, John Fiske to "shed tears profusely" over the grave of Gellert while he is busy tracing out his Sanskrit origin we will proceed to call attention to another theory, according to which at any rate some of the myths and legends may have originated independently at different places and among different peoples.

As has been shown before, the natural laws engaged in mental development are the same everywhere and make the mind react in the same way when furnished with the same stimuli. It reacts correspondingly even if the stimulus-object is somewhat different and so one may take the place of another. For instance in the Tell myth at one place it is an apple, at another a nut, and at still another a coin that is shot off from the head of a dear person who in one case is a son, in another a servant, and in still another a relative. But in all cases the bow and arrow are used. Now, could not this myth have originated independently in places where archery was a well-known art and much time spent in perfecting it? Or take the case of Gellert. The dog has been man's faithful companion from time immemorial. He has watched over him diligently night and day, and man has learned to appreciate and even love him. Would it be necessary under such circumstances to trace the origin of this myth to Sanskrit in order to find an explanation for it? Would it not be just as feasible to assume that it originated independently among different peoples who had much to do with this faithful companion? It seems that if mind works according to definite laws in the same way everywhere, the myths could easily arise everywhere there the conditions and environment allowed it. But where the external conditions and circumstances did not favor it, or where the mental level was not adequate for such a response the result was not obtained. That is to say where the stimulus could not be given or where it could not be responded to for lack of appreciation on the mental side, the myth could not arise. That this is true in other mental fields is a well-known fact and there is no adequate reason why it could not be true in the formation of myths also.

The objection may be raised that this theory excludes the possibility

people to another by means of intercommunication and contact, and that it necessarily separates one race from another, while it can be shown that races have had intercommunication and taken over mental products from one another to a greater or lesser degree. This may be granted, but contact and intercourse themselves are no guarantee for the transmission of traditions, because those who should adopt the mental products of another people, must have all the paraphernalia necessary for such a transaction *e. g.* their mental and physical conditions must be favorable. They must have what Herbart calls the apperceptive mass, otherwise the adoption would be impossible. But with this granted there is only one step to the independent development, namely, that the right kind of stimulus be given, just as there is only one step in the transmission, namely, that the material be presented for adoption, although this step may be somewhat shorter and easier to take. Therefore, an outright borrowing is not considered very ingenious by students of mythology to-day. Says Brinton (10):

> "I have already referred to the strange similarity in the myths of savage nations far asunder in space and kinship. The explanation of this is not to be found in borrowing or in recollection from a common, remote unity; but in the laws of human mind. The same myths are found all over the world, with the same symbolism and imagery, woven into cycles dealing with the same great question of human thought. This is because they arise from identical psychic sources, and find expressions under obligatory forms, depending on the relation of man to his environment, and on the unity of the mental processes throughout the race."

And John Fiske (23) writes, although he seems to favor the theory of central origin:

> "The religious myths of antiquity and the fireside legends of ancient and modern times have their common root in the mental habits of primeval humanity. They are the earliest recorded utterances of men concerning the visible phenomena of the world into which they are born" . . . "In primitive society the consideration of the same phenomena leads to a number of typical associations which differ from our own, but which occur with remarkable regularity among tribes living in the remotest parts of the world."

These typical associations differ from our own, because the amount of knowledge which underlies them is not the same in both cases, but their regularity assures us that if the same stimulus be given and if the mental development be along similar lines the result will be the same. Therefore wherever the bow and arrow were known, and wherever the dog associated with man there was a possibility for the Tell myth and the Gellert myth to arise, if the mental development was adequate for such a response.

That two so widely separated peoples as the Brahmans and the Mexicans should have borrowed from one another the story of the fish-god that sows the seed of man, seems incredible. Furthermore, primitive people did not migrate as much as they are supposed to have done, for, as Brinton (11) says:

"It is proved by the distribution of the oldest stone implements that primitive tribes were not generally migratory and had little intercourse with their neighbours."

## III. Nature Myths, Their Origin and Import

As soon as man began to reflect upon what happened around him, he began also to form his own explanation and opinion of these phenomena, as he saw them. That he did not come to the same conclusion as modern man may well be expected. Copernicus, Galileo, and Newton had not yet expounded the revolutions of the heavenly orbs and formulated the laws of nature; Linneus, Harvey, and Darwin had not yet classified, described, and explained the natural world; philosophy had not yet begun to raise any doubts, and man was left undisturbed to ponder upon the problems that demanded solution around him. Consequently he gave his own explanation of the natural objects and the natural phenomena as he saw them.

### A. *Natural Objects*

1. *The Tree.* Among those objects which early attracted man's attention the tree seems to have occupied a very prominent place. This would be quite natural, for, if the Simian ancestors took to the trees after having emerged from the primeval ocean, these played a great rôle in the sustenance and further development of the species. Seemingly from the support which the trees gave man in his early existence, even if he never lived in trees, as seems to be the present tendency to believe, he developed elaborate theories about life-trees and world-trees of which the Scandinavian world-ash Yggdrasil is the most prominent and minutely worked out. This world-ash

has three roots, all in the underworld. Near the fountain of Mimer lay the germ of Yggdrasil. From here it grew up and sent out its roots, one towards the North, to the fountain of Hwergelmir in Nifelhel, the second towards the South, to the fountain of Urd, and the third to the fountain of Mimer in the middle of Ginnungagap. From these fountains the tree received nourishment and strength, and it grew to an enormous height and spread its branches far and wide. Upon the network woven of the fine threads from the three roots, lay the foundation of the underworld, in the first cluster of branches was Midgard, the home of man, located, and in the second Asgard, the home of the gods. The top of Yggdrasil overshadowed Odin's hall, while the branches towered far and wide over all the worlds. The tree was ever green, its leaves never withered, and it supplied gods and men with many useful and indispensable things.

But all good things have their enemies, and so Yggdrasil. Close by the wondrous tree, near the fountain of Hwergelmir, there lived a dragon, Nidhug, which ceaselessly gnawed the roots, assisted by countless worms. They knew that when the tree died, the downfall of the gods was at hand. But the Norns or Fates who are the servants of the gods, sprinkle daily the tree with holy water from the Urdar fountain and thus maintain its healthy condition.

The tree is a creation of the gods who endowed it with many characteristics. It contains the elements of all past, present and future generations; the primordial elements of each individual man budding and maturing upon its branches are carried away by the storks which are Lodi's birds to those who yearn for a new being.

The Babylonians developed a somewhat similar idea of a world-tree which, according to Sayce (69), was at first the cedar but subsequently the palm. This tree rested on the earth with its roots far down into the abysmal deep, where Ea, the god of wisdom, presided, and nourished the earth with the springs and streams which forced their way upwards from the roots to the surface of the ground. Zikum, the primordial heaven, rested, as it were, upon the overshadowing branches of the mighty stem. Within it was the holy house of Davkina, the great mother, and of Tammuz, her son, "a temple too sacred and far hidden in the recesses of the earth for mortal man to enter."

Thus, the poets of the Eddas and the Eridu portray the same mythological fancies and draw pictures which in many cases resemble one another. But the sacred tree of the Babylonians was more than a world-tree. It was also employed, says Sayce

"in incantations and magic rites which were intended to restore strength and life to the human frame. It was thus essentially a tree of life and the prototype and original of those conventional trees of life with which the walls of the Assyrian palaces were adorned."

In the religion of Zarathustra the tree of life is called Horn and grows, according to Zend-Avesta, by a spring upon a mountain. It is king of all trees. Ferverdin, who is the door-keeper of paradise, like Riswan in the Moslem saga, and his followers guard it against the attack of Ahriman who wants to possess it. This tree assures resurrection to those who die in faith and has the power to reveal thieves and murderers before they do any harm.

Kalevala, the Finnish national poem, tells of a mighty oak which sprang from an acorn planted by Wainamoinen and which

"raised itself above the stormclouds dimming the sunlight, hiding the moonbeams and causing the stars to die in the sky until a hero alarmed at its growth appealed to the mother, the windspirit, who sent forth a dwarf grown into a giant whose strength overcomes the oak. It falls and its power to bestow good is only then discovered."

Unlike Yggdrasil this world-tree is overcome by its enemies, but this is for the good of mankind. Like the Babylonian cedar or palm it is used in incantations and magic rites to bestow power and happiness.

That man originated from trees was the belief not only of the ancient Scandinavians where Ask and Embla were turned into human beings by the gods and where the elements of each individual buds upon the branches of Yggdrasil, but also of many other people. Hesiod (42) tells us that Zeus made a brazen race of ash trees and Virgil (82) writes:

"These woods were first the seat of sylvan powers
Of nymphs and fauns and savage man who took
Their birth from trunks of trees and stubborn oaks."

Ormuzd gave soul to a plant which had first grown up single but afterwards divided into two, Moschia and Moschiana, who became the parents of the race. And the Mexicans believed that their ancestors had come from the seeds of the sacred *Mariche* palm.

Closely related to the world-tree is the belief in the possibility of climbing to heaven in a tree. If the heaven, the land of the gods, were located in the upper branches of that tree upon whose lower ones the earth had its place, why was it not possible to climb to that place of happiness and bliss in a tree? Many races far separated in time, space and culture said it was, and their answer has reached the nursery tales of our own times.

That trees were alive, have spirit, sensations, and feelings, was the belief of almost all ancient peoples Frazer (25) has shown that many tribes even to this day believe that to cut down a tree is to dispossess a soul and commit matricide. The Fiji Islanders will never eat a cocoanut without asking: "May I eat thee, my chief?" And the young among the Thompson Indians of British Columbia prayed to the sunflower root before eating it.

Prayers of all kinds were offered to the trees. Their worship ranges from the mere adoration till an intimate life-connection with them like that of the Dryads of Greek and Roman mythology and the Druids of Celtic who would suffer even unto death, if their trees were cut down.

Almost every nation seems to have developed a special cult around a special tree aside from regarding all trees more or less sacred. This singling out of a particular tree is, however, of a much later date than the general belief in the spirituality of all trees which is more generic.

2. *The Sun, Moon, and Stars.* The important place which the sun, moon and the stars have occupied in man's life from the very earliest time, is seen in the early development of astronomy and astrology. The sun has dominated the day, the moon the night, and every being has had his star which directed his life from the cradle to the grave; and the Magi followed such a star from the far East to the manger at Bethlehem to pay homage to the new-born babe. The temples from gray

antiquity, in Egypt, Babylonia, Greece, and Rome, down to the cathedrals in the Middle Ages were built according to astronomical considerations, and the very word orientation is derived from the custom of looking at the sun-rise.

The relation between the sun and the moon has always been regarded very close but not by any means fixed all over the world. Primitive man's idea of sexualizing everything was carried out here, too, but not uniformly, for among one people the sun is regarded as masculine and the moon as feminine, while among others the opposite holds true. Max Müller (54), loyal to his language idea of mythology, traces the word moon back to Sanskrit and finds that *Mas* is masculine, and Harley (41) concludes that "the very word moon is masculine and like Wordsworth's child father of the man." For our purpose it matters not whether the word sun or moon is masculine or feminine as such, for the gender of a word will often change in the same language. It is the idea that underlies the conception that is of psychic importance, and this idea is fundamentally the same whether the word moon or sun is masculine in one and feminine in another language, for they are never of the same gender in the same language.

"In early philosophy throughout the world," says Tylor (79), "the sun and moon are alive and as it were human in their nature." The Egyptian Osiris and Isis were brother and sister but also husband and wife and identified with the sun and moon. In the Northern mythology the sun and moon are two beings, daughter and son of Lodur and Mimer's daughter Natt (Night) and chosen by the gods to drive the golden chars which the artisans of the underworld had made to light the world. The ancient Mexicans believed that when the old sun burnt out and left the world in darkness a hero sprang into a huge fire, descended into the shades below and arose deified and glorious in the East as the sun (Tonatiuh). After him another hero sprang into the fire but it had now grown dim and he arose only in milder radiance as the moon (Metztli).

When the Greek philosophers and astronomers maintained that the sun was only a hot ball swinging around in the sky, they caused great outcry and disturbance in the minds of both the aristocracy and the populace. And Tacitus (77) tells of a German chief who, when the Romans prepared to drive the people from the land, turned to the sun and invoked it to look upon the vacant soil.

The native races of the Americas give more or less veneration to the sun, bring their sacrifice and smoke their pipes in its honor. The Delawares regarded it as second in rank to the twelve great Manitus. The Sioux Indians regarded it in appearance the maker and preserver of all things. The Natchez of Louisiana had a complete sun-worship in accordance with which the whole state was modelled. The priest was the chief called the sun or the sun's brother. The sun was both the ancestor and the founder of the dynasty of the Incas of Peru who reigned as its representatives and almost in its person. They took wives from the virgins of the sun's convent and their descendants were the solar race and the ruling aristocracy.

Although the sun occupies a very prominent place in the minds of primitive man, its worship is by no means universal, as some authors want us to believe. It seems to be somewhat restricted to the regions where its beneficial influence was mostly felt and where the changes occurring in nature with its departure and arrival were most manifest. The feelings of the Massogetae of Tartary who sacrificed their horses to the sun that freed them from the dreadful miseries of the long winter must have been quite different from those of the people of central Africa who dreaded the rise of the morning sun. The ancient Scandinavians did not include the sun and moon as such among their deities and their worship is quite unknown. But where the sun was less worshipped the moon seems to have had a greater place in the people's mind. The savages of Brazil regulated their time and their festivals and drew their omens by the moon. The tribes of the south central part of Africa watch for the new moon, hail it and hold their festival day. The Congo people fell on their knees at the first glimpse of it and exclaimed: "So may I renew my life, as thou art renewed." And the Hottentots used to dance and sing all night at the new and full moon addressing all their desires for prosperity to it

As the ruler of night when the influence of gloom and quietness, aided by leisure and emotional events, could exert itself to the utmost, the moon may well be expected to have had a greater effect upon man's ideas than the sun. The moon could be looked at, meditated upon in special way and observed in all its changes. In Greece it fell in love as Selene with a beautiful youth, Endymion, who was taken up with it and afterwards became the man in the moon for the Greeks. Here we have the prototype of that mysterious face which has caused so much speculation and which is met with in all parts of the world, in some form or other. Baring-Gould (6) thinks that the "Jack and Jill" jingle owes its origin to the old Norse tale of two children who carried a bucket of water on a pole and who were taken up by the moon. The same idea goes through the old German story of the man who gathered wood on Sunday and as penalty was transferred to the moon where he stands as a fair warning. Similar legends are found in many other places and are plainly of Jewish or Christian origin.

But there are not only human beings in that heavenly orb. Some people have seen other things there. In India the story runs that a hare in a famine offered to give up his flesh to a Brahman who in return for his willingness immortalized him by drawing his face in the moon. A similar legend is found in China, and a modified form of it among the Hottentots where the moon sent a hare to tell the people on earth that just as it wanes and waxes so the people shall die but rise again. But the messenger forgot the last and most important clause for which the moon got very angry and tried to kill the hare with a hatchet. It missed him but split his lip and in return got its face scratched by the hare.

The stars are not only personified but personal action is ascribed to them. They are even declared to have lived on earth. The aborigines of Australia consider the Orion as young men dancing corroboree and believe that an ancient race was transplanted to heaven before the present race came upon earth. The Eskimo held that all stars were in olden time men and animals transplanted into the sky. The Pleiades was called the dancers and the morning star the day-bringer with more than a superficial meaning. An Iowan told of a man who gazed at a star until it came down, talked to him and directed him to a place where there was much game.

The belief in the influence of the heavenly orbs upon man's life is as strong as it is universal. The stars guide his destinies and th[illegible] cradle to the grave. But not only man is affected. The moon corrupts the flesh, destroys the wood, grain and vegetables, causes the changes in the weather and influences the crops.

### B. *Natural Phenomena*

1. *Eclipses.* Eclipses had a terrifying effect upon the mind of primitive man and caused many to us peculiar stories to be invented as an explanation of the dreadful phenomenon. Thus the Chiquitas thought that the moon was hunted across the sky by a huge dog, caught and torn until the blood dyed its face red. In order to drive away the monster the people used to raise a frightful howl and lamentation and shoot across the sky. The Caribs thought that Maboya, hater of all light, sought to devour the sun and the moon and therefore danced and howled in concert all day or all night to drive him away. And the Peruvians imagined an evil spirit in form of a beast eating the moon and therefore raised a frightful din and beat the dogs to join in the concert.

The same idea is also found on the South Sea Islands where the sun and the moon are supposed to be swallowed by an offended deity but who was induced by offerings to eject them again. In Sumatra the one eats the other but the inhabitants are able to prevent it by a tremendous noise In Hindu mythology two demons Rahn and Ketu devour the sun and the moon respectively. These are also described in conformity with the phenomena: Rahn is black and Ketu is red, and the usual din is raised to drive them off. But as they are only heads, their prey slips out as soon as swallowed. Another version of the myth says that Indra pursuing Rahn with his thunderbolt, rips open his abdomen so that the heavenly body gets out again. Ancient Mongols and Chinese make the same kind of clamor of rough music, gongs, and bells to drive off the monster. And the Siamese said in regard to the Europeans' ability to predict the time and extent of an eclipse that they knew the monster's mealtimes and could tell how hungry he would be.

The Romans flung firebrands into the air, blew trumpets and clanged brazen pots and pans in order to save the moon. And when the soldiers made a mutiny against Tiberius, their plans were frustrated by the moon which suddenly languished in the s[illegible] for clouds came up and hid it and the mutineers saw that the gods had turned away from their plot.

But not only external influences or causes were considered as effecting an eclipse. Internal causes or changes in the sun or moon themselves were also believed to bring about this phenomenon. The Caribs thought that the moon was sick hungry, or dying. The Peruvians imagined the sun angry and so hid her face in total darkness to bring the world to an end. The Hurons fancied the moon sick and arranged a rather boisterous concert in which men and dogs participated in order to bring about its recovery. In Cumana it was believed that the sun and the moon married but because they had a will of their own they began to quarrel and fight with the result that one of them was wounded. In such a quarrel the Ojibwa endeavored to distract their attention from one another by a tumultuous noise and so stop the quarrel and fight.

The changes of day and night, summer and winter, spring and fall—light and darkness, heat and cold are very closely connected with the eclipse-belief. The one is overcome by the other only to return with renewed strength to conquer the oppressor and to free and gladden the heart of trembling humanity, once more asserting the power of light, truth, righteousness, and life.

2. *Winds.* The winds that break the forest, shake the rocks, and penetrate man have also caused much wonder and speculation. Æolus of old held the winds imprisoned in his dungeon cave and tuned his harp after them, and when the winds rustled among the leaves of the trees, people heard Æolus play his harp. The Mani of New Zealand ride upon the winds and imprison them in their caves, but the West wind is too strong and too cunning, for he escapes, hides himself in his own cave and dies away. In India the Maruts, the storm-gods, assume after their wont the form of newborn babes and perform the mythic feats of the child of Hermes, tossing the clouds over the surging sea. Boreas, born of Astraios and Eos, causes the people to tremble with chills and hurry to their shelter. He chases the birds from their summer haunts to other regions and ties in asbestine bonds the soil and the waters.

The Polynesian believed that the wind-gods lived near the great rock which serves as a [illegible] held within themselves hurricanes, tempests, and all destructive winds and employed them to punish such persons as neglected their worship, wherefore in stormy weather large offerings and liberal presents were brought them by penitent devotees who were either in danger themselves or had friends in danger. The four winds caused a great mythic development among the natives of America in which they are personified as four brothers, or mythic ancestors, or divine parents of mankind.

3. *Thunder and Lightning.* The strong effect of thunder and lightning upon the mind of primitive man is seen in the myths all over the world. Rig-Veda sings Indra's glory and ascribes to him the "feats of the thunderbolt" He is also called Indra of the thunderbolt. He smote Ahi and poured forth water upon the earth. When he hurls his thunderbolt men believe in the brilliant god and pay him homage. Twashtar made his glorious bolt. The North American Indians had much to tell about the thunder-bird, as had the ancient Greeks of the eagle of Zeus and the Scandinavians of the hammer of Thor. The Assiniboins have seen this wondrous bird and the Dakotas could show his footprints, the thunder tracks, twenty-five miles apart, near the source of St. Peter's river. The Ahts of Vancouver talked about the mighty bird Tootooch dwelling far off in the sky, the flap of whose wings caused thunder and whose forked tongue is seen in the lightning. The Mandans heard in the thunder and saw in the lightning the flapping wings and flashing eyes of that awful bird which belongs to or even is Manitu, the Great, himself. The Ahts say that there were originally four of these great birds but Quawteaht, the great deity, entered a whale on which they fed and enticed one after the other to swoop down when he seized them and plunging into the sea drowned them. The last of them was, however, too strong so he spread his wings and flew to a distant height where he still remains, though he sometimes visits the earth. The Dakotas spoke about an old, large bird which begins the thunder and whose velocity is great. He is wise and kind and never does any harm. But the thunder is imitated and carried on by smaller, young birds which cause the rumbling noise and the duration of the peals. These are mischievous and will not listen to good counsel and therefore do some harm sometimes but as a [illegible]

This explanation of the thunder and lightning which is so prominent among the Indians, especially of North America, is found also in other places. Thunder and lightning may be the messenger of the god who lives far on high and so needs a messenger, or else the god itself as in the Finnish poetry where he speaks through the clouds and shoots his fiery darts. When it is dark in his lofty abode he strikes fire and we hear the noise and call it thunder and see the sparks and call them lightning. The Hindu Indra hurls the thunderbolt with his bow, the rainbow, just as Uko in the Finnish saga and both smite their enemies with these arrows.

Closely connected with the thunder and lightning is the rainbow, as we might expect. It constitutes, as we have seen, the bow of Uko and Indra. The Israelites called it the bow of Jahwe, the Hindus the bow of Rama, and the Lapps the bow of Tiermas, the thunderer, who slays with it the sorcerers that hunt for men. Zeus stretched it down from heaven as a sign of war and tempest, or it was Iris, the messenger between gods and men, that came down. In Scandinavia it was a bridge for the gods to travel upon and in Germany the souls of the just go over it to paradise.

4. *Creation, Vegetation, Reproduction.* A beginning of things has probably not been conceived of by all races in their primitive state. But quite many have had at least some conception of it, and these seem to have keenly appreciated the dilemma of postulating an absolute creation. The law of causality exerted early its power upon mind and primitive man solved the problem in his way.

Among those elements which man postulated as primeval was water the most prominent and universal. The primeval ocean with its boundless extension and its necessity for the maintenance of all life appealed early and powerfully to man's power of imagination. In the water all possibilities were present. But this boundless extension was sterile, until a creative power acted upon it and fructified it. In Genesis the spirit of Elohim brooded over the face of the waters. In Kalevala the eagle floated over the water and hatched land. And in the Eddas the fountain of creative Wisdom mingled its contents with the streams of the two other primeval fountains and produced the primordial elements

Some Athapascans held that a mighty bird descended to the ocean and instantly the earth arose and remained on the surface of the waters. The same bird called forth all animals and man. The Quiches believed that there was in the beginning nothing but water, quiet water, in which the mothers and the fathers slept until Hurikan, the mighty wind, passed over it and called forth the earth. And the Zunis supposed that the great All-father impregnated the water and from this union everything came into existence.

The Hebrews postulated a god who existed and in the beginning created heaven and earth, and all things with them by the power of his word. So easily could not the ancient Scandinavians dispose of the problem. For them there was in the beginning Ginnunga-gap, a yawning gulf whose depth no eye could fathom and three elements or powers, the cold, the warmth, and the creative wisdom. This Ginnunga-gap or chaos is the empty space in which the world was created. Hindu, Greek, and Teutonic mythology agree in making this the first postulate. They also agree in making water the primordial element. The cold waves from the North, the world of mist and darkness, flowed into this chaos and formed the primeval ocean out of which the world has arisen. The life-giving principle which was necessary for the production of this world was the warmth and came from the South. This met the cold waves in the chaos and partly melted their icy element and formed thereby the vital drops out of which the world was made, the seed of Yggdrasil, the world-ash, and the like. The creative wisdom shaped and guided this first formation as well as the following. The three fountains, Hwergelmir, Urd, and Mimer, contain the vital sap necessary for the world-tree to grow and develop.

When the cold and the warmth met in the chaos there originated, also, from this fusion the primeval cow, in Teutonic mythology called Audumla. By her actions she brought forth, also from the watery element, the world-giant, Ymer, and the progenitor of gods and men, Buri (Gayomant), who seems to be the personification of the wind, the father of all the other storm gods. Of Ymer's body is the visible world made.

The idea in Greek mythology is somewhat similar. In the [illegible] Erebus mist, water, and Night, darkness, and

Earth were produced. Earth gives birth to Uranus, heaven, which envelops her and gives birth to Oceanus, the Titans, etc.

In Hindu mythology a later version makes the Brahma lay the mundane egg in the bottomless chaos, hatch it himself and then come from the very same egg himself and of its contents make the visible world. In the Upanishads (80) Sat (=that which is) is made the source of all things. Sat produces progressively heat, (heat leads to) water, (water leads to) earth, and by a mixture of these everything else is produced. There is an intimation that Brahma is identical with Sat as well as with Atman.

Whatever may have been the primitive notion of the Hindus their thoughts soon centered around a trinity, Brahma, Vishnu, and Siva, but these are in modern Hinduism only three forms or characters of the same deity. Brahma is the creator, Vishnu the preserver, and Siva the destroyer. They are sometimes represented singly with their special emblems, sometimes jointly in one body with three heads. Their origin is rather nebulous. In some Parunas they are represented as sprung from a female source Adi-Sakti (the original powers). In other that Adi-Sakti produced a seed from which Siva was born and he became the father of Vishnu, and in still other that a flower of the Tamarosa plant (water lily) sprung from the navel of Vishnu gave birth to Brahma who laid the mundane egg mentioned above.

There seems to be both in Hindu, Teutonic, and other mythologies a dim conception of an all-father who was uncreated and by whose influence the world was created, but this conception was so vague that more tangible means was resorted to for an explanation of the visible world.

The god or the creator is often referred to as the father more or less literary of all things and as such associated with one or more feminine beings. Exceptions to this occur, however, and the god brings forth offspring without the help of a mate, as for instance the Satapatha Brahmana's story of Mani, the Phœnician ancestor of the race, and the first Zoroastrian being, split up later by Ahura Mazda.

All primitive creation myths abound in sexualities. Uranus and Gaea had marital relations which Cronus, their son, once prevented and by his ...

tiful Afrodite. Cronus married his sister Rhea and swallowed all his children except Zeus who punished his father for his crime. Zeus indulged in so many love-affairs with goddesses and mortal maidens that his reputation has become quite bad. Hera's jealousy caused him to conduct his courtships often secretly and in disguise.

The same loose family idea goes through the Teutonic mythology. The gods and goddesses intermarry not once only but many times and produce a large number of offspring. And the Hindu deities are still worse as far as their morals are concerned. Brahma seduced Parvati, the wife of Siva who avenged himself by striking off one of his heads He married his own daughter, Sarasvati, but not daring to satisfy his incestuous passion under human forms, he changed himself to a stag and her to a hind. Again, as Prajapati, he offers violence to his own child.

In Teutonic mythology Odin, Vile, and Ve participated in creating man by transforming two trees Ask and Embla into human beings. The trees grew up from seeds which Yggdrasil had dropped into the earth. What took place at the creation of the first man takes place at the creation of every man. The fundamental part of every being buds, blossoms, and ripens into fruit on the branches of the world-overshadowing ash whence it is carried to women who want to be caressed by children. Vile, the lord of the fire-drill and the inflamer, places it in the bosom of the mothers.

One of the most remarkable creations of mythic fancy is the world-mill Crotti which the primeval artisans built in the underworld. The upper mill-stone is turned around by nine giantesses who walk along the edge of the earth and push a monstrous beam. With the mill-stone the firmament is also moved around.

By the friction of the mill-stone the holy fire was originated and with it the god Heimdal who thus is the holy fire impersonated. He was born in the image of a child by the nine giantesses who turn the world-mill by pushing the beam which is thus the first fire-drill. Vile, the inflamer and the supervisor of the world-mill, gives the same fire-drill to man after his cr[illegible].

### C. *Notes on Nature Myths*

With this cursory perusal of the objects and phenomena of nature which interested primitive man and which irresistibly attracted his attention and called for some kind of explanation we may have gained a background on which to base an interpretation and conclusion as to his procedure and method in dealing with the external world. Let it not be understood, however, that the foregoing includes all the objects of interest and wonder to primitive man, nor that it arranges them in order of importance, because that is not so, since everything under the sun has, at some time or other, been the cause of speculation and interest. But those things enumerated may serve as examples of what busied his mind and therefore represent the trend of thought he usually followed in dealing with the world around him. That the explanations which he made do not concur with those given in modern time or that he did not follow the same kind of procedure in reaching his conclusions, ought not to cause any surprise or make us reject them, because the different conditions can not be compared. To deny originality and power of invention to primitive man would be to give ourselves away completely, for if anybody was original and inventive he was. But it is very difficult for modern man to divest himself of the preconceived idea of superiority and very easy for him to look down upon preceding ages as inferior. Inferior they may be but only relatively not absolutely; for if we judge each period or age in the light of the one just preceding, as we must do in order to be just and fair to all concerned, the conclusion to which we come, may be quite different, and the age of primitive man stand forth as the most remarkable and progressive of all. The historical setting must never be overlooked in judging the merits of a certain age. To compare twentieth century B. C. with twentieth century A. D. and then exult over the enlightenment of the latter at the expense of the former would be exceedingly unfair. Neither can we compare the people of each period with one another without taking the social standing as well as the personal character into consideration. A university president and a woodland farmer of to-day belong both to the twentieth century but to two different classes of people both in regard to social standing and mental development; but both are men and both may be Aryan.

That the influence of natural phenomena upon the mind of primitive man was great is certain, but still we might overestimate this influence or emphasize one at the expense of another, perhaps equally important, in our attempts to unearth the different opinions that have come down to us, presumably from gray antiquity. No doubt many of the interpretations imposed upon our remote ancestors and ascribed to them are wrong and products of the imagination of comparatively modern times. Have we not in our endeavor to grasp the meaning of the records of primitive man's thought made them more intricate, complex, and too one-sided than they really are? There was a time and that time has hardly passed yet when almost every myth was considered a solar myth and almost every hero a solar hero just as if nothing but the sun existed for primitive man. Why all other phenomena and objects, and many of them concerned man more closely than the sun, were left unnoticed nobody seems to offer an explanation for, and still Mahaffy (52) remarks:

> "I do not suppose that any ancient Aryan possessed with good digestive powers and endowed with sound common-sense ever lay awake half of the night wondering whether the sun would come back again."

And when Sir George Gray (quoted by Tylor, 79) told some of the Australian natives about countries where the sun never sets during part of the year

> "their astonishment knew no bounds, and an old man said 'Ah that must be another sun, not the same as the one we see here;' and in spite of all my argument to the contrary the other adopted this opinion."

According to this theory Tell is a solar hero; Oedipus is the sun himself who slays his father Laios, the Night-demon, and in the evening is united to Jokasta, the Dawn, who gave birth to him in the morning, just as the Vedic Indra, the sun, born of Dahana (Daphne), the Dawn, whom he afterwards marries. To this Vedic story the Greeks, says Cox (14), added the rest "in order to satisfy a moral feeling." Thus Oedipus is exposed like Paris upon Ida, the earth which in this case is Caetheron,

> "because the sunlight in the morning lies upon the hillside. The Sphinx is the storm-demon who sits on the cloud-rock and imprisons the rain.

. . . The omniscient sun comprehends the sense of her dark utterings and destroys her, as Indra slays Vitra bringing rain upon the parched earth.''

The Erinyes are the personification of daylight

''which reveals the evil deeds done under the shadows of night. The grove of the Erinyes is the fairy net-work of clouds which are the first to receive and the last to lose the light of the sun in the mornings and evenings; hence although Oedipus dies in a thunderstorm yet the Eumenides are kind to him and his last hour is one of deep peace and tranquillity."

With all due respect for the sun and its influence upon the mind of primitive man, as well as for all curious interpretations of primitive legends that have come down to us, this solar interpretation seems nevertheless too narrow to be accepted. It leaves too many other phenomena out of account, although they may have been just as striking and mysterious to man in his early habitat as the sun. We have shown in the foregoing that the moon, although perhaps lesser in glory, has had a greater influence upon man's mind and career than the sun. The moon-lore is more prominent than the sun-lore in all parts of the world.

The tree seems to have been a very interesting object for primitive man, for all over the world we find temple groves, sacred groves, trees actually worshipped, world trees, sacred trees, life trees, etc., beside a great tree-lore. Quantz (62) makes an attempt to correlate all this with the theory that man or man's progenitors once upon a time lived in trees which therefore play such a great rôle in his life. Whether this is so or not the fact remains that the tree has occupied a very prominent place in man's thought from the earliest time.

If it is permissible to judge from present day data to past experiences the returns to President Hall's (38) Questionnaire on Fear show a very interesting fact. The objects most feared at present time are the lightning and, next in order, the serpents. Why lightning and serpents should be feared so out of proportion to their real danger is a very interesting question and President Hall suggests, and Quantz takes up the suggestion, that this may be atavistic and due to the arboreal condition of primitive man, because in that kind of life he was more liable to injury both by lightning and snakes, since light-

explained and the thing explaining are older than their new interrelation, their mythological significance.

But as soon as he became conscious of the fact that something grew just as he did he drew the conclusion that it must have life as he had, or be as he was, with the same sensations and feelings as he had; when he became conscious of the fact that something moved he inferred that it must have the same power of locomotion as he had; and when he consciously saw that something acted in the same way as he, purposely, he concluded that volition and purpose guided the action as it did his own. Primitive man did not need to have more than these three factors growth, motion, and purposive action, in order to explain the whole universe after his fashion. From those cases in which these were manifest he inferred that everything else must be in the same way endowed with the same properties with which he and other objects were endowed. Therefore, when a tree grew, a river flowed, and an animal acted, they were prompted by the same powers that made him grow, move, and act. Says Hewitt (43) "By primitive man all motions and all activities were interpreted as manifestations of life and will." That some things did neither grow, nor move, nor make any other sign of life did not cause him to doubt his own interpretation. For, says Hewitt, "things animate and things inanimate were comprised in one heterogeneous class, sharing a common nature." He, as Baldwin (4) says of the child, projected himself into the external world and strictly interpreted it in terms of himself. For this reason he understood the winds as either personifications of some individuals nearly related as in the myths of some of the Indians, but more often they were the breath of a mighty being who was sometimes friendly, sometimes hostile, as among the Australians. The noise which the birds make when they rise from the ground resembles somewhat a distant thunder, especially if they are large, and primitive man seized the opportunity and said that the thunder was the flapping of the wings of a large thunder-bird. Thus he explains one phenomenon with the help of another.

In this way the natural objects were personified or endowed with the same powers and attributes as man. Behind the natural phenomena were placed powerful beings who acted in them. Sometimes the natural objects were handled by powerful individuals as the sun and the moon in the Norse mythology. All natural phenomena were at some time or other attributed to somebody, although this does not appear plainly in all cases, and all natural objects were sometime endowed with human faculties. Or, as Klaatsch (48) maintains, the mental process was the other way around and persons were elementarised, instead of the elements being personified. In this way there is a difference between the natural objects and the natural phenomena.

Everything had thus a soul of its own or perhaps better shared in the soul common to all and was prompted by the same motives. Everything was subject to the same feelings and emotions. Friendship and hostility existed among the different entities or beings that bepeopled the universe. The sun pursued the moon and the moon the sun, somewhere in a pleasant, somewhere in an unpleasant mood. Everything was subject to the same weaknesses and could be helped by concerted action. When adversities or accidents happened to man in his business, when something went wrong or contrary to his plans, the cause was always sought in the hostile feelings of some beings who had to be warded off either by friendly action or by force of arms. The antagonists must either be placated or conquered in some way. For this reason sacrifices were offered, tricks were played, and the best results obtained in the best way possible.

Thus we see that the interpretations which man made of the phenomena around him were derived from his own life. Activities which he was engaged in were attributed to things around him, the heavenly bodies above him, and, later on, to the more specific gods. What he did others must do, as he felt others must feel, and in the same circumstances he lived others must also live. So completely analogous was his reasoning, so completely deductive was his logic that it took him a long time to think of anything different from himself. Says Hewitt (43):

"All things, therefore, were thought to have life and to exercise will, whose behests were accomplished through orenda—that is through magic power, reputed to be inherent in all things. Thus all phenomena, all changes, and all activities were interpreted as result of magic power directed by some controlling mind."

This mind was considered the ultimate source of all things

and consequently inhabited all things and made them powerful agencies for good and for evil. We find the same tendency in the child of to-day. The stone that breaks the doll, the door that hits the head, or the chair that tumbles over are all living agencies, conscious of what they are doing, and a certain satisfaction is felt in seeing them punished. But whether this is a remnant of primitive thought or caused by the surroundings is a question difficult to settle.

The idea that this supersensuous agent, the soul, was a separate entity which could leave the body and journey to lands far off and return with wonderful tidings originated in all probability in the dreams. In these dream-excursions the soul met other souls, conversed with them and came back to tell the story. That this phenomenon had a remarkable effect upon the plastic mind of primitive man is certain. To it may be traced not only the belief in a soul as a separate entity, but also the belief in spirits with whom man could communicate and who could inspire and influence him as well as reveal the unknown.

The idea of immortality may also have got a strong impetus from the same source but it may have grown out of the struggle for existence unconsciously. The mysterious is always a great notion-producer and when reality is not known most everything is mysterious.

These facts given there is but one step to the formation of gods who were also made by primitive man in his own image, with attributes and characteristics like himself. This step was taken when man felt his inability to cope with a given situation and perceived stronger and more mysterious powers than his own. That the gods were or became greater than he was a necessary result of his inability to master a given situation, and of the feeling of dependence which man got during his long infancy and which Schleiermacher (39) defines as religion, as well as from the idea of co-operation developed later in life. It was necessary to anthropomorphize the gods in order to understand them, and this tendency is clearly illustrated in all ancient as well as in the more modern religions And we are not yet able to divest our gods of the human attributes which our ancestors gave them. Perhaps it is impossible, for we may not be able to conceive of any gods except in anthropomorphic terms.

Therefore, the personal is the most important part in primitive religion and without this there could be no religion, and the relation between man and his gods was purely personal. Fear which has played and still does such a large rôle in the explanation of the origin of religion and the creation of the gods, is surely only a secondary factor and at best only one among several. Fear of the gods could not have created the gods, as Brinton (10) rightly says, but conscious volition and purposive acting is the foundation upon which the gods are reared. They could not have been feared before they had been conceived of even if the Lange-James theory of emotions be applied to them. We must not confuse the origin of religion with the origin or first conception of the gods. It might therefore very well be a strong factor in the origin of religion but have nothing to do with the origin of the gods. And as Klaatsch says, "the fear of the influence of a powerful dead man, especially a shaman, is the embryonal stage of fear of god present in the highest religious system." There is thus the personal element present in the beginnings of all religions and in the first conception of the gods. And Robertson Smith (72) has shown that fear did not enter into the primitive religions to any great extent. This is a comparatively modern idea and belongs especially to Christianity. The idea of sin was not clearly developed in primitive times, and punishment could consequently not be conceived of. The gods were feared mostly for their own sake because they were capable of both good and evil. With the endowment of conscious volition given, fear certainly entered in as a factor in the development of religion as well as of worship.

There is still another factor which played a great rôle in the origin of the gods and their worship, namely *desire*, purely selfish and generically human. This desire was manifest in man's wanting to get away from an enemy, to reach safety and to satisfy his own wants and pleasures. For instance, when he was down on the ground and an enemy appeared, is it too much to assume that he manifested a distinct desire to get back to the tree where he felt more at home and where he could ward off the enemies more easily? This is not purely conjectures either for in the primitive religions the tree occupies so large a place which is difficult to explain without recourse to some such theory as this. Even if man's progenitors took to the ground before he became man, he might nevertheless have resorted to the tree in times of danger habitually and thus begin to worship it first of all objects that afterwards entered into his religious consciousness and became a part thereof. This desire was of course not limited to the idea of reaching the tree but extended to other fields and activities as well. It prompted man to obedience and submission and gave him a powerful stimulus to try to obtain whatever his desire led him to.

But when primitive man had his gods ready, they felt as he did, but in a greater measure; the same motives that prompted him, prompted also them; and the same desire that stimulated him, stimulated them. Nothing that man felt, did, or was, or was stimulated by, was too low or too high for the gods. Furthermore, man's social organisations and institutions were also ascribed to them. As he was born into this world, so were they. Each god had his father and his mother, just as man, although there was some difficulty in accounting for all of them, because they were so many and their pedigrees somewhat uncertain. How the first one came into existence was a difficult problem to solve. The Hebrews assumed that they were eternal, the Scandinavians that the creating principle was eternal and that the gods sprung from that in due course of time. Almost invariably man was created by his gods in some way or other. The gods were married, had families, and were led by sexual desire to commit horrible things which we must not call crimes, because they were committed by the gods. That all these conceptions were derived from man's own domain is certain. Such as he was, such were also his gods, and as he lived, so did they also live. They were a mere copy on a large scale of himself. They were real and entirely human but belonged to the realm of the unknown and consequently gave room for the play of the human imagination.

If man was mortal, his gods were mortal and doomed to die, if nothing intervened. But to prevent their growing old and subsequent death a remedy was discovered. Thus the Scandinavian gods ate of Iduna's apples, the Hindu gods drank the immortal Soma, and the Greek gods partook of the divine nectar to gain this prerogative. When this elixir was denied them they grew old and feeble. But in the long run this elixir was not strong enough to maintain them. They died, anyway, died a natural death, not only Pan, the great, whose death was publicly announced and greatly lamented, but the rest of them, Zeus, Odin, Hera, Freya, and those left are in the process of dying. This terrible catastrophe could not take place at once but was brought about by a slow process which kept pace somewhat with the development of man's thinking and reasoning power, for when man begins to think and reason the gods tremble in the jaws of death.

In this process we may distinguish three or four different stages more or less clearly marked out. In the first conception of the gods the object was the god and the god was the object. Later on the gods were imminent in the object or phenomenon which thus came to represent them. Still later the gods disappeared entirely from the object and took up their abodes far off in the cloudy heavens or on the lofty mountains from where they still visited man now and then and still acted in the phenomena. At this stage most of the more carefully worked out theogonies were shaped and preserved. But what brought about this change? Simply the fact that man began to doubt his first inference and became more conscious of the significance and right meaning of the objects and phenomena. And since the god-idea was so strongly associated with his own self that he could not get rid of it, the only thing to do was to remove the gods to a place where his present knowledge could not reach them. As a result of this removal of the gods they became dimmer, and again as a result of this symbolism arose, since man could not live without some visible or tangible representation of his gods. An object of some kind was chosen to represent the gods or symbolize them. Thus animals, trees, stones, etc., were chosen as symbols of the gods and worshipped and revered as such.

That this change was slow, slower in some people than in other, is certain. But the human mind which always yearns for more light but reluctantly accepts it when it comes, was set agoing and could not be stopped in its onward march. Fetichism, the gods of the individual as contrasted with the gods of the race, had to give away for the gods of the community or race as soon as the individual became subordinate to the society and his actions permissible only in so far as they served the common good, although both may have originated from the same idea. In the struggle for existence which not even the gods escape, the weaker gods had to give away for the stronger, that is to say for those of the stronger society, and in themselves absorbed the characteristics of the weaker which were closely related to theirs. In this way they became a condensation of characteristics and a differentiation of these as well as of functions. A particular field of action was assigned to each one. This process continued till the monotheistic stage was reached in the human culture and the evil gods degraded to demons or evil spirits.

The unity of the godhead, says Jevons (44), was logically implied from the beginning in the conception of personal power, greater and higher than man. This may be so, but it may also be regarded as a natural development in the struggle for existence, or as Nietzsche has more aptly expressed it: "The Will to Power," which is a far better expression for the same idea. This includes not only a mere existence with which no normal being is content; not only a will to live in Schopenhauer's sense, but to live abundantly, to power. And as soon as and in the same degree as this will to power becomes conscious in the human race the downfall of the gods is certain. One by one they are eliminated and the remaining become an abstraction too far away for the human being to reach.

## IV. Hero Myths, or Culture Myths

As has been said before no clear line of demarcation can be drawn between the nature myths and the culture myths because they overlap somewhat, as for instance in the Mexican theory of the present sun. But there is a large number of distinct culture myths, and it is to these that the Freudian method of psycho-analysis has been especially applied. Thus Freud himself has analyzed the Oedipus myth and given the clue to the Prometheus and Hamlet myths later worked out by Abraham (1) and Jones, respectively. Rank (63) has analyzed a large number of hero-myths and gives a "Durchschnittssage" of all the hero-myths as follows:

"The hero is the child of prominent parents, mostly the son of a king. Difficulties precede his birth as abstinence or long infertility or secret intercourse of the parents in consequence of prohibition or obstacles.

During the pregnancy or even before comes a prediction (dream, oracle) which warns for his birth and threatens mostly the father with injury. As a result of this it is decided to expose the new-born child mostly upon the request of the father or a person who represents him. As a rule he is given over to the water in a small casket. Then he is rescued either by animals or poor people (shepherds) and nourished by a female animal or a simple woman. Grown up he finds his prominent parents in a very circumscribed way, avenges himself on his father, is recognized and becomes great and famous.''

Not all hero-myths correspond to this description in all particulars but in general the fundamental traits in all of them conform to this. This universality of general features has led to the assumption that they must spring from a general source and develop in a certain way, and that the same psychic forces are at work in all of them.

But not only have the culture myths as such been invaded by the Freudians. The same process has been applied to literature in general and to poetry in special, as well as fine and plastic arts. Thus Freud has analyzed Jensen's Gradiva (33) and Leonardo da Vinci (34); Graf has analyzed Wagner's Der Fliegende Holländer (35); Rank, the Lohengrin saga (64); Abraham, Giovani Segantini (2); Phister, Ludwig von Zinzendorf (60) and so forth, so that this kind of literature is steadily increasing.

It would perhaps be well to give the outlines of the analysis of the Oedipus myth as given by Freud (28) as an example of both the subject matter of the sagas and the factors at work in the formation of them, according to the Freudian psychoanalysis. To be sure not all culture myths seem to correspond to this one in particulars but that depends mostly upon the fact that certain parts of the myths may in some cases be better concealed than in others and therefore not so easily seen.

''Oedipus, son of Laios, king of Thebes, and of Jocasta, is exposed as infant, because an oracle had told the father that the still unborn child should be his murderer. But he is rescued and grows up as son of the king of another country (Corinth). Being uncertain as to his parents he asked the oracle and received the answer to shun his home, because he was destined to murder his father and marry his mother. On the way from his supposed home he met king Laios and killed him in a precipitated strife. He came then to Thebes where he solved the riddle of the Sphinx who blocked the way and as a reward was elected king by the Thebans and given Jocasta as wife. He ruled a long time with peace and dignity and had with his wife two sons and two daughters.

But a plague broke out which caused the Thebans to resort to the oracle again and received the answer that the plague would cease when the murderer of Laios was banished from the country."

"The treatment of the case consists now in an unfolding step by step—comparable of the work of a psycho-analysis—that Oedipus himself is the murderer of Laios and son of the murdered and Jocasta. Grieved by his act, unknowingly committed, he blinds himself and leaves his country."

Judging from the fascinating influence which this tragedy and others similar to it has exerted upon the human mind during all ages Freud concludes that they must contain something which calls up a related feeling in all of us. This he finds in the sexual emotions which he judges from their universality and strength to exert the strongest influence and to take often unassumed directions. Moreover, he concludes that "it was decreed for all of us perhaps to direct our first sexual emotions to the mother and the first hatred and violent wish to the father." And Abraham (1) remarks that "the tragedy contains the realization of two intimately connected childhood- or dream-fancies: the fancy of the death of the father and of the love relationship to the mother." Abraham leaves out one very important component of this constellation which is very closely related to it, namely, the wish to become great which is manifest in all culture myths. The sagas contain thus a wish-fulfilment, as Riklin (67) has so amply shown, acted out in fancy. This wish may persist into adult life and animate all endeavors to acquire new positions and make new expansions, and take expression in dreams and reveries. That neither the Oedipus myth nor anyone else of the culture myths are actual occurrences, nobody will contend, I presume. But, if they are not real in reality, they are nevertheless real in the fancy which has constructed them, and as such they portray the innermost feelings and emotions of the soul.

As is seen from the above and from other myths analyzed by the Freudians as well as from the culture myths in general, this kind of myths is a comparatively late upshoot in the human history. In the following we will trace their origin and development in the individual and society. That all culture myths are strongly emotional is a self-evident fact. They must therefore originate in strong emotions which take expressions in them. To my mind it does not make so much difference of what kind these emotions are, only they fill the requirements and are adequate to the purpose. They thrive to be sure best in neurotic persons because they are more emotional.

### 1. *Sexual Emotions: the Child vs. the Parents*

If we go back far enough on the phyletic scale we come to a time when there were only two motive powers in the world; Nutrition and Reproduction, and to these all other activities owe their origin. Of these two factors hunger may be said to be the most primitive, because it appeared first on the phyletic scale. But as soon as there was nutrition there must also be reproduction of some kind or other and thus sex in the wider sense is almost if not quite as old as nutrition. As to the relative strength of these primordeal impulses there can be no question. The sexual impulse as exemplified in life is by far the strongest. Among the animals where the impulses have a greater freedom to exert their influence than in man we have many illustrious examples of this fact. The male spider which carefully watches for hours every move the female makes in order to catch the most opportune moment seldom survives the successful execution of his intentions and if he does escape minus a leg or something else he is just as eager and daring the next time. Other animals will watch without food even at the point of starvation, prompted by their sexual impulses, for an opportune moment to enjoy their gratification often at the expense of life. In man the sexual emotions are so checked that they no longer exert their real strength but even there they sometimes take on tremendous proportions. Says Ribot (65):

"Sexual instinct remains the center around which everything evolves, nothing exists but through it. Character, imagination, vanity, imitation, fashion, time, place, and many other individual circumstances or social influences give to love—as emotion or passion—an unlimited plasticity."

And again:

"The sexual impulse is fatal, blind, not acquired, anterior to all experience,"

and Spencer remarks (74):

"This passion which unites the sexes . . . is habitually spoken of as though it were a simple feeling whereas it is the most compound and therefore the most powerful of all feelings."

The age of puberty is the natural time for these impulses. At this time new ideas are formed and new associations of previously existing ideas are brought about. The individual self begins more than before to exert its rights and demand recognition. The opposition between the individual self and the social self becomes more marked and it is apparent that a great revolution is going on. The importance of this period is recognized by different races in the very elaborate tribal initiations into manhood and womanhood, that take place at this time. A conscious awakening of the self is taking place. But says Ribot:

"observation seems to show that, at a much earlier age, in the fifth and sixth year there are apt to occur (quoting Dallemagne) 'unconscious genital impulses provoking association of ideas which frequently serve, in later years, as a *substratum* to our sentiments and volitions.' "

Bell (7) goes further than this and shows that what he calls sex love exists between boys and girls of three years of age and upwards. And Freud (29) maintains that

"a newborn child brings with it the germs of sexual feelings which continue to develop for some time and then succumb to progressive suppression which in turn is broken through by the proper advance of the sexual development and which can be checked by individual idiosyncrasies. Nothing is known about the lawfulness and periodicity of this oscillating course of development. It seems, however, that the sexual life of the child mostly manifests itself in the third or fourth year in some form accessible to observation."

This period comes out prominently in der kleine Hans who at the age of three developed a strong sexual interest which manifested itself in various ways. Jung (46) has also given some illustrations of this, especially the Anna case.

The objects of the emotions of tenderness and love are in the first place the parents themselves. Then it may branch out to other persons, especially brothers and sisters or playmates. It is a striking fact that the sexual feeling or love is generally directed to the opposite sex, although there can be no conscious appreciation of the anatomical differences between the sexes. Bell has shown this very plainly and Freud strongly maintains that the first object of our love was the parent of the opposite sex. Der kleine Hans showed a strong predisposition for his mother just as Elizabeth von R. and Anna did for their fathers. The same thing is seen in mythology. A male child mutilates his father when he is going to embrace his mother, as for instance Cronus and Zeus. Schidlof found that the aborigines of Australia believed the child to be jealous of the father if not placed in a certain position with the mother (70).

This predisposition can not, of course, consciously materialize itself owing to several circumstances. In the first place the cause of attraction is unknown; and in the second place it goes against other feelings which manifest themselves and demand recognition. To postulate any moral consciousness at this age would be absurd. The children have their own moral standard as far as they have any at all and can therefore not be judged by the social code.

But this feeling of aversion toward the same and attraction toward opposite sex takes nevertheless some definite form in the child's mind. It may be clothed in symbols and concealed in words but shown in acts with a distinct meaning. The meaning of the symbols which are often very striking, may be vague, forgotten, or perhaps unknown and must be suggested in order to be recognized and remembered, but if this is done produce a feeling of certainty which reality alone can produce.

This phenomenon is perfectly normal, says Freud. It may take on abnormal development in neurotic and mentally weak children but in normal children there is no danger. It is an expression of the great psychic forces which are formed and transformed in the soul. After a while these forces subside, in a word are suppressed, and another period in the child's life begins. This period which Freud calls the "latency period" is of prime importance for the child's mental development. The sexual life and emotions are as it were latent, hence its name, but

"it is during this period of total or at least partial latency that the psychic forces develop which later act as inhibition on the sexual life and narrow its directions like dams. These psychic forces are loathing, shame, and moral and aesthetic ideation masses. . . . Surely education contributes much to it. In reality, however, this development is organically determined and can occasionally be produced without the help of education."

"These constructions so significant for later personal culture and normality are apparently brought about at the cost of the infantile sexual emotions themselves, whose influx has not ceased even in the latency period, but whose energy, wholly or partly, has been switched off from sexual utilization and applied for other purposes.''

This process is called sublimation and furnishes powerful components for all cultural accomplishments. The mechanism of this sublimation is built up by the fact that

''the sexual feelings of these infantile years were on the one hand not utilized, since the functions of procreation are postponed, which is the chief character of the latency period, and on the other hand they were in themselves perverse, *i.e.*, emanated from erogenous zones and born of impulses which could only call forth sensations of unpleasantness in the course of the development of the individual. They call therefore up psychic forces which counteract them and which build up the above mentioned psychic dams: Loathing, Shame, and Morality, in order to suppress effectively the feelings of unpleasantness.''

Binet (29) was the first to point out that the persistent influence of a sexual impression mostly received in early childhood often shows itself in selection of a fetich which may be of very diverse kind. And Freud points out that the sexual symbolism which uses the hand, foot, mouth, etc., as sexual objects ''seems often to depend upon sexual experiences in childhood.'' These symbols were used in the same sense in ancient times.

The sexual impulses have played a great rôle in man's life from the very earliest times, as is seen in the myths of various peoples. A hasty reference to the religious life and ideas of primitive man, and even highly civilized peoples, will suffice to show this fact. Even if no pure phallic worship ever existed, which is doubtful, the part sex played in primitive religions is so prominent that it can not be overlooked.

Having thus shown the prevalence, strength, and direction of the sexual emotions in the child and primitive peoples and touched upon the forces which work for morality in the individual, the next step will be to show the forces at work in the suppression of these impulses and the result thereof.

## 2. *Development of Moral Ideas: The Individual vs. the Society*

Waitz (85) has very properly said:

''Whosoever would arrive at a just conception of man must not consider him exclusively as an individual being, for man is, as was well observed by Aristotle, a social being; as an individual he cannot be fully understood."

And Storfer (75) says:

> "The individual—if we can at all imagine the splendid isolation of such a fictitious presocial being—creates no ethics and for him is no ethics created. He has, however, in the experience of pleasantness and unpleasantness, within certain limits, a more or less reliable leader for his behavior, a damper on his impulses, but first the living togeth[er] creates the values good and bad."

Thus, as soon as two or more individuals began to live togeth[er] the freedom of each was necessarily restricted by the rights of the other which must be respected and honored if the com[-] munion was going to be of mutual benefit. For this reas[on] there was established some rules of conduct, perhaps uncon[-] sciously at first, which later developed into the written and unwritten codes which constitute the standard of behavior [in] a given community. What the society as such has come [to] regard as right or wrong the individuals have had to subm[it] to and their behavior has been judged accordingly.

There has, however, always been certain individuals or class[es] of individuals who have been as it were immune and who ha[ve] had privileges, either on account of their position or on accou[nt] of their profession, which have not been accorded other ind[i-] viduals, for instance the dancing girls and temple prostitut[es] connected with religious observance whose business has alwa[ys] been regarded as proper by the society in which it has flourishe[d].

In the evolution of ethical ideas pleasantness and unpleasan[t-] ness, modesty and shame have played a great rôle, indeed a[re] their very roots. We find them even in the animal world whe[re] the female coyness must be regarded as a kind of modest[y] which however is overcome when the sexual emotions prevai[l]. This shows that modesty and sexual emotions are very closel[y] related and that the former is the offspring of the latter whic[h] arise simultaneously with consciousness of true sexual lif[e]. The facts certainly point this way at least in the human bein[g]. The child has no modesty except in so far as he has been taugh[t] by his elder associates, until the time of puberty when the sexu[al] emotions with their accompaniments begin to assert themselve[s]. Perez (57) has shown that modesty may appear very early i[f] the sexual desire appears early. And Hall and Allin (40[)] think that "it is hard to find all the causes of modesty and shame, but it is certain that very much of what is best in religion, art, and life owes its charm to the progressively widening irradiation of the sexual feelings."

It seems therefore fair to assume that modesty began to arise when consciousness of sex began to develop an awareness of that anatomical and physiological difference between the individuals which is necessary for the propagation of the species and the complete happiness of the individuals.

The idea maintained by Sergi (71) and others that the feeling of modesty and shame is the result of clothing, does not differentiate between the physiological and the anatomical modesty, the former of which is by far the earlier, and is not substantiated by the facts, for people like the Guanches, Puris, South Sea Islanders, etc., go about absolutely naked or nearly so and still possess a highly developed sense of modesty. And Waitz relates that "some Indians on the Orinoco where both men and women go about naked, were at first ashamed to wear clothes as it seemed to them indecent to appear before strangers unpainted."

That clothing has an intimate relation to the feeling of sex is beyond question. The dress is often regarded as a strong sexual stimulant. Westermarck (86) has emphasized this side of the concealment idea and regards modesty as the result rather than the cause of clothing, which was adopted, he thinks, to give prominence to the sexual organs, not primarily to conceal them, for "savage men and women in various ways endeavoured to make themselves attractive to the opposite sex:—by ornamenting, mutilating, painting and tattooing themselves," and the time especially chosen for this purpose is the age of puberty.

The custom to clothe or conceal any part of the body and especially the primary and secondary sexual characteristics had in all probability a psychic origin in the sexual emotions. It must be remembered that physiological modesty precedes anatomical and that its primary factors existed and were discovered long before any ornamentation and clothing were invented. Furthermore, the clothing of primitive peoples in most instances does not fulfil the idea of concealment and consequently can not serve as a factor averting shame. It is probable that this, like ornaments which indeed it is, had only a sexual signifi-

cance in the first place and served
came to be propagated as a powerf
of a specific end. Then when and
as environment and climate as we
clothing necessary and its adoption
tive, this feeling of modesty was
with clothing, which although a
played an important rôle in the
rôle which must not be underesti
secondary.

The place which sympathy has t
moral instincts has been emphasiz
maintains that parental care is the
which they have risen with all "ac
sense of duty, the feeling of self
both the tender and the manly ideal
(22) has pointed out the psychic co
he says

> "that an unconscious sexual dispositio
> every sympathetic feeling and that whe
> the same or opposite sex) the unconscio
> transference. If the unconscious succe
> pleasant to the conscious either in pure
> ated, concealed form (respect, gratitude,
> then sympathy arises between the two. I
> negative to the always positive unconscio
> pathy which is, in relation to the strengt
> degrees up to disgust."

Freud's (31) Dora case is a typi
exception.

Some emphasis has been laid up
a powerful factor in the developm
moral ideas. Richet (19) came to
arose from the sense that somethin
And Crawley (15) has shown th
be looked upon by primitive man w
and consequently was forbidden
prohibition "occurs at puberty" wh
the idea that danger from the othe
period." Havelock Ellis (19) mai

arousing disgust is the ultimate and most fundamental element in modesty."

The moral concepts which are based on the emotions of approval of the good and disapproval of the bad or wrong, pleasantness and unpleasantness, have developed according to natural selection and are states of mind useful, as a rule, to the organism which accepts them. Wrong implies pain and good assures pleasure and benefit to the same organism. Consequently what furthered and helped him along in the struggle for existence came to be looked upon as good and had the approval of this same organism while that which caused him pain or was a hindrance in his development was looked upon as bad and wrong and disapproved of. The feeling of pleasantness and unpleasantness, of help and hindrance, lies thus at the bottom of all moral concepts which could not, however, arise before the individual with his pleasantness and unpleasantness became subordinate to that of the group or society.

Those who regard the intellect as the source of moral concepts, hold that moral emotions arise only in consequence of moral judgment and that the character of the emotion is determined by the predicate of the judgment. To this Westermarck replies: "moral emotions cannot be ascribed as resentment or retributive kindliness called forth by moral judgments" and "moral judgments could never have been pronounced unless there had been moral emotions antecedent to them." The moral judgment does not involve any self-interest, at least not openly, which shows that it is a characteristic of moral concepts as such, from which we may conclude that the emotions are felt disinterestedly. But the moral judgments are only apparently impartial, not fundamentally so, because we have greater obligations to some people than to others. They aim, however, at impartiality as well as at generality at least within a given group of people or a tribe, but they can never lay claim on universality, because one group may have developed along wholly different lines from another and therefore have wholly different moral concepts.

In early society as well as in smaller societies of to-day there is practical unanimity in regard to what is good and what is bad, what is right and what is wrong. For this reason such a solidarity has come about that each member considers all others like himself and regards any harm or good done them as done to himself. The pleasantness and unpleasantness is the same for the individual and the group. In larger societies where the membership and the complexity in organization is greater this solidarity and oneness is not so conspicuous and perhaps not so necessary in the struggle for existence but it is there nevertheless and at an adequate stimulus is ready to assert itself.

Therefore, whether an act shall be approved of or not depends upon the moral concepts and these again depend upon the lines along which a given society has developed. If the society has said that a certain kind of clothing is necessary in order to conform to the standards of modesty and morality, the casting off of that kind of apparel will be stigmatized as wrong and treated accordingly. The act may be harmless in itself but nevertheless cause disgust and disapproval and make the society inflict punishment upon the agent. The liking and disliking of the neighbours affect man easily, especially if he is of an emotional nature. Thus society is the birthplace of the moral consciousness, and the tribal customs are the earliest rulers of duty and can therefore not be regardlessly interfered with. This is seen in both primitive and modern society. The Greenlanders conceived of the idea of virtue as something pleasing to the Europeans when they tried to acquaint them with their own moral conceptions. And Westermarck (86) remarks: "The Bedouins of the Euphrates make no appeal to conscience or the will of the gods in their distinction between right and wrong but appeal only to custom." In the lower stages of civilization, especially, custom is a tyrant that binds man in adamantine fetters and threatens the transgressor with public disgrace and bodily suffering. "Custom," says Westermarck, "is fixed once for all and takes no notice of the preference of the individuals." Customs do change, to be sure, but by recognizing them I recognize their binding force and make myself one of their supporters. But since not all persons are alike there is sure to be some opposition in the individual against some custom which interferes with his feelings and personal interests. As a result these must be disregarded if the custom exerts the stronger influence, as is generally the case. The stronger the feelings and interests are and the more powerful the customs and traditions are the more intense will the conflict be that takes place in the person's mind between the personal feelings and interests and the social customs and traditions, and the more far-reaching the results. And so powerful is the influence of moral approval or disapproval exerted by society in its customs and traditions that under ordinary circumstances the personal feelings and interests will have to give away without regard for the consequences. These may not even be taken into consideration at all. The whole process may be infra-conscious or only partly conscious, but even if the conflict is fully conscious and the struggle between the individual's emotions and the opinions of society is carried on with a full meaning of its import, the individual generally follows the ordinary course of events and regards customs and traditions the superior masters and the indignation and resentment felt by society toward such an act as he is inclined to commit too powerful to cope with. The import and far-reaching consequences of this conflict, from which we can infer the strength of both the individual emotion and the custom and opinion of society as well as the seriousness of the struggle, are seen in the torments of the conscientious soul who has yielded to his emotions and committed an act disapproved of by society. In extreme cases sanity is in the balance, life is not worth living, and not even death is a perfect consoler. The feeling of public resentment and disapproval is much more potent and conspicuous than that of approval. The latter is always taken as a matter of course and very seldom publicly recognized while the former occupies a very prominent place in every society. The individual merely disappears in the steadily flowing stream until he commits an act that obstructs the smooth flow and sets society aghast. Then he is at once noticed and the proper consequences follow.

The fact that a man who transgresses the customs and traditions of a given society is punished even to the extent of being excluded from the society or tribe and even put to death undoubtedly impressed itself upon the mind of the individual with all the might and rigour possible. Westermarck (86) and Steinmetz (quoted by Westermarck) have related many instances where expulsion was meted out to those who committed a sexual offence. Van Wrede (quoted by Westermarck) states that after a period of three days which was given the offender by the Bedouins of Hadhramaut in which to escape, any man could

kill him wherever he found him. Spencer and G
Frazer (25) tell the same story in regard to
except in their cases a special board of execut
erally appointed by the elders. And many cas
in which the sense of duty and allegiance to
society was so strong that the offenders gave th
justice and if sentenced to death but let go fr
of execution on that day presented themselves re
penalty for the offence. That this would be imp
a strong sense of guilt and an unshaken belief
bility of the customs and traditions of the s
Even those who, in a well-meant effort to rai
higher level and inject new ideas into the old f
regarded public opinion, have often fallen pre
unlimited and never-to-be-forgotten or disregard
shows the influence which society has had over
life and thought, especially the more emotiona
always apt to take the customs and traditions
than others. They adhere strictly to what is pr
as right and avoid conscientiously everything reg
But it is just these emotional beings who most
into conflict with the standards of society. The
strong and therefore difficult to control and th
proved of by society in which they can find
narrow. Moreover, those who have a strong e
have also a strong imagination and these two su
impulses and ideas which not seldom come at
society. As a result they have to choose betwe
out their impulses contrary to the customs and
take the consequences, or else suppress them.
it might mean death, expulsion from society, or
for life; in the second it might mean a cramp
its consequences. It is needless to say that bo
been taken; and it depends upon the individual
stances at the moment which course will be
particular case. If the public disapproval and
sciousness of the individual are strongly devel
circumstances favor it he chooses to inhibit
but if the public disapproval and the mora

are weak and other circumstances favor it he acts them out. The result in each case depends upon his own make-up as well as upon the circumstances under which the act was committed. As a rule, however, the impulses are not acted out but struggled with and suppressed, merely because it would cause greater pain to act them out. The whole question falls thus back upon the idea of seeking pleasure and avoiding pain. In this way a great deal of our emotional and intellectual life is suppressed and never allowed to take form in our daily life. How much of our mental life shares this fate is of course impossible to say. It depends upon the individual himself and the society in which he lives. But what is thus suppressed soon leaves the field of consciousness. In course of time perhaps the struggle between the emotions and public standards, the process of suppression, becomes unconscious and takes place as a matter of course, on account of the continued allegiance to the prevailing custom. In most cases there may however remain a fleeting experience of something coming up in consciousness but as strange and unconventional is forthwith thrust back into the subconscious again and is soon forgotten. Freud and his school have repeatedly pointed out that we forget sooner a painful experience than a pleasant and this is corroborated by Peters (58) and others. Our daily life is full of the same thing. We try to expel from our consciousness all unconventional thoughts and unpleasant experiences and exhort others to do so too. If we otherwise mean anything by all this there must be something in it.

This process of expelling and forgetting the unpleasant and unconventional can also be explained on physiological and evolutionary grounds. A stimulus that has caused pleasant reactions tends to be repeated while one that has caused unpleasant tends to be avoided. This causes in the case of a pleasant reaction more and closer associations as well as easier passage along the lines laid out, while an unpleasant experience which does not tend to be repeated must necessarily cause fewer associations and have a more difficult passage along the nervous paths, and are consequently crowded out of consciousness faster and more easily than the pleasant ones. Moreover, the organism as a whole reacts more favorably to pleasant stimuli than to unpleasant and therefore makes them predominant in con ness. As a result they are more easily recalled. Jung (4 shown that the reaction time of the unpleasant stimuli is longer or wholly absent which shows the predominan pleasant associations. This holds true both in regard to p and moral unpleasantness because, as Ribot says, there difference between moral and physical pain as such, mora being

> "the beginning of mental disorganization just as physical pain beginning of physical disorganization. . . . Everything th presses or impedes them (the needs, appetites, the physical or tendencies) is translated into pain,"

and treated as such.

Prince (61) and Chase (13) seem to think that we as the unpleasant feelings with something in order to drain and so rid ourselves of them. If that were the case there not be any question of suppression because they were out and not suppressed. But this can hardly be so b we do not as a rule associate a painful experience or t with anything for by so doing we strengthen the pain a drain it. If we think of something else after a painful ence it is not because we want to connect the pain with because we want to crowd the painful experience out minds, of consciousness, suppress it, if you please, by readily formed associations. Furthermore, the experime Aschaffenburg (3), Jung and Riklin (67) which seem to that the closer we get to the margin of consciousness th associations are there of form and less of content, sho that our association of the unpleasant with something the content kind and not of form, because we are never conscious than when an unpleasant experience occurs to therefore we tried to get rid of our unpleasant experien associating them with something else, that something strengthen the same experiences and keep them longer i sciousness and more vividly as well as tend to call th whenever this something occurred to consciousness again. this happens is one thing and may be recognized but w it is the general mode of procedure is another, and it see seems not to be.

### 3. *The Freudian Conception of Consciousness.*

The foregoing discussion will necessarily turn our attention to the Freudian conception of consciousness and especially to that part of it which is called the "subconscious" or "unconscious" which is, of course, not strictly a Freudian term. Freud includes in the mechanism of the subconscious 1, traces of past experiences which may be recalled to consciousness at will; 2, processes like the conscious but unconscious to the subject, and 3, complexes which have sunk so far below the threshold of consciousness as to be incapable of recall to consciousness at will. But instead of dividing the subconscious into three parts or layers Freud includes the first two under a common head, the Vorbewusste, the foreconscious, because consciousness in both of them is an exception and not a rule, but they are capable of being recalled, and gives the third the name Unbewusste, unconscious proper, or preconscious, as it is also called, because its contents have sunk beyond voluntary recall and are made up of complexes foreign to our immediate customs and habits of thinking.

The ideas and complexes of the preconscious or unconscious proper are the background of our mental life. They do not penetrate into consciousness, however strong they may become, but since they have a certain dynamic character, and grow active at the least provocation, they always exert their influence upon consciousness which manifests itself in various ways, as for instance in the execution at a prescribed time of a suggestion made in a hypnotic state, and the errors in memory and speech, forgetting names, etc., and hundreds of cases in abnormal and hysterical persons.

The foreconscious which is made up of recent pleasurable experiences in conformity with our customs and habits of thinking and in which most of our thinking goes on, serves as a censor upon the preconscious ideas and complexes and suppresses them as soon as they try to enter consciousness. The ideas contained in the foreconscious may become conscious either by voluntary recall or by adequate stimulation, but the foreconscious admits only that to consciousness which is in conformity with its contents. All the rest is thrown back into the preconscious from whence it came, that is to say, is suppressed. But the preconscious ideas are dynamic and hence active and can not very readily be gotten rid of. They try to get into consciousness indirectly, take on another form, disguise themselves in some way or other in order to escape the censuring action of the foreconscious.

Freud thus looks at the psyche dynamically and postulates two systems of energy representing the preconscious and the foreconscious. The first system is sensory and is discharged by a sort of blind impulse which he calls wish and which is seen everywhere in the effort to seek pleasure and avoid pain. It tries to represent pleasure as vividly as possible and sometimes reaches the level of hallucinations by a retrograde process which tends to dramatize the complex. The second system of energy is quite different and develops slowly with the individual. It seeks satisfaction in motor discharges which function automatically in a simple situation but in a more complex develop thought as a substitute of activity. It takes account of both pleasant and unpleasant stimuli but an idea which would cause too much unpleasantness the foreconscious represses into the preconscious.

These two systems of energy which, as Freud thinks, constitute our real psyche, produce all psychic phenomena. The energy tends always to discharge and such ideas and complexes as possess a high degree of tension "tend to press through and become material for the perception of consciousness" (28). But since some ideas and impulses have been suppressed into the preconscious because they were accompanied by pain the foreconscious will not allow them to pass through or to discharge their energy for the same reason for which they were suppressed in the first place. They can not be suppressed continually, however, because they are dynamic. Their energy is therefore transferred to other ideas or complexes which in some way resemble them and which thus symbolize them without having their painful aspect. These are not recognized on their face value as carriers of the forbidden energy and escape therefore the foreconscious censor. In this act of Verschiebung the emphasis is laid on something quite different from that to which it really belongs. The emotional value is thus retained but the process takes time and the surrogate does not appear until some time afterwards.

In the effort to present the contents of the unconscious to

consciousness several ideas or traumas are condensed into one, the so-called act of Verdichtung, which is thereby "überdeterminiert." It may contain for instance in a dream one part of the body of one person and another part of another person, with the head of a third, the voice of the fourth, and the manners of a fifth, etc., until the necessary components of the picture are presented.

This theory holds necessarily to the conservation as well as summation of energy, and that no psychic process is ever lost in our neural mechanism. There are nervous stimuli which are too weak to overcome the synapses but still are able to cause same neural changes. These reinforced or allied to some stronger stimuli will ultimately cause some effects on the mental life. It makes consequently no difference how strong the foreconscious censor is the energy from the psychic effects stored up in the preconscious will in some way influence our mental life. In normal cases this is done by way of sublimation and diversion to all fields of mental activity. But in abnormal cases the energy breaks through more easily and therefore influences the mental life more directly. In neurotics whose bringing up has given them some ideas and conceptions which conform to the social status, the foreconscious objects so strongly to the preconscious energy that the whole mental make-up becomes unbalanced.

The Freudian conception of consciousness seems very mechanical and highly artificial but lays claims to be demonstrated every day, for who would write on a public blackboard all the "freisteigende Einfälle," all the thoughts and ideas, that come to consciousness a single day, and which are not allowed to remain there a single minute unless we are moral and intellectual imbeciles but are immediately suppressed? The partly conscious foreconscious got a glimpse of them but straightway they went down to the place from where they came unless we are degenerates in which case we harbor them and take pleasure in so doing, but then they cause no longer pain but pleasure.

### 4. *The Influence and Expression of the Subconscious*

The suppressed ideas, complexes, and emotions are not for ever inactive or dead. They are present in some form or other and always more or less active. Ideas which are apparently

forgotten and unconscious are for instance in the hyste
unconscious in the sense of only disposably present—as
thing which one does not think of—but they are only
mitted. The hysterics are in regard to them in a peculi
tion of knowing and not-knowing which in reality is
more or less conscious not-want-to-know, as Freud puts
235), and the feeling of opposition between this know
not-want-to-know must be overcome. Their admittance in
sciousness is sure to bring relief to the patient and res
normal life. Sometimes these emotional ideas are so fa
in the recesses of the psyche that it takes hard work a
searching to find them but they nevertheless influe
mental life and a decided relief is experienced as soon
are let out. All psycho-analytic therapy shows this.

These suppressed feelings and emotions sometimes fir
outlet in bodily symptoms into which the mental or psyc
is transferred or converted.

The root of the neurosis, says Freud (30), is in th
hood when man is more emotional and plastic than
other period. But if the affective life of the child is sub
into other lines of activity, there is little danger th
experiences will have their emotional tone strengthene
to cause injury. The energy is being used up for oth
poses. This is what usually happens in all normal
When the emotions reappear in consciousness they have
another garb and are used for other purposes than
tended for. This sublimation of the suppressed emotic
their application to other ends is a drainage upon their
which is thus made useful in all walks of life, for it is
sible to say how much of our poetry, our fine and plas
of our religious, sociological, philanthropical, and philos
conceptions is due to these suppressed emotions. But
well-known fact that all poetic, literary, artistic, r
geniuses are of a more or less emotional nature. As
their imaginary powers are strong and the preconsciou
greater chance to exert its influence because more pro
is likely to occur in them. Then, under certain condi
in childhood, in sleep and reverie or in special emotion
breaks, when the power of the foreconscious is lower
preconscious is able to discharge its energy more freely.

day-dreams and reveries the emotional tone is always present and colors the whole situation. The dream and the poem are in their external appearances very different but both conceal their real significance behind the manifest content. Goethe's "Heideröslein" and "Gefunden" show a very insignificant and harmless patent content, but in them, says Voigtländer (83), "have the two fundamental forms which a man's relation to a woman can assume, found expression most wonderfully precise." And the same author remarks that the real poems are diary pieces of feelings, reports from the subconscious, and remain on the transition between the expression and repression, nature and art; their anchorage in the latent experiences is mostly still too plain. The analysis of Goethe's latent experiences and the above mentioned poems would in all probability lead to his relations to Friederike and Christine.

But not only poetical expressions are stimulated by the subconscious. Nietzsche (56) remarks that "the conscious thought of a philosopher is secretly led and escorted by his instinct," by which he means nothing else than the influence of the subconscious. Leonardo da Vinci (34) shows plainly how the subconscious dominates his whole life. He is very unstable in his habits and complains over a lost life in which he had not accomplished what he ought to. The same is true of Giovano Segantini (2). Says Voigtländer (83):

> "All flashes, all conceptions come from the subconscious,—the conscious is not creative, only arranging, sifting, presenting. The material for the thought comes from the unconscious, the wishes, instinct, experience. . . . Not what one says or writes is the essential—the logical connection is loose and only apparent—behind stand wishes, interests, the whole past, and generally the whole concrete personality of the individual,"

and these are the powerful factors in man's life. The laws of association which are so convenient and useful in explaining certain phenomena, are at bottom not able to explain anything. Beyond the ideas on the surface of consciousness there lies the all-determining past of human experience, feelings and emotions, stored up in the human soul. The energy behaves like itself wherever it is found. Nothing happens anywhere without a cause, and if the whole story were known from beginning to end, cause and effect would undoubtedly connect the procedure like links in a chain. The mental impressions will remain like splinters in the flesh until they are removed or made harmless.

Of special interest in this connection is the r
dreams, day-dreams, and myths. Abraham's
that myth is nothing but an overcome infantile
collective dream of the race, was somewhat antic
ner (quoted by Havelock Ellis, 20) who said:

"If we bear in mind how intimately poetry and
nected with myth, we encounter the surprising fact t
of these highly important vital manifestations is not t
action of waking mind, but in sleep and that the chief
of productive imagination is not to be found in the
but in the phantasies of dreams."

And it is a well-known fact that the Greeks
excellent myth-makers wasted much time in wai
Truly has Jewell (45) spoken when he said:
had a great effect upon the history of the world

The argument of the Freudian school that th
formation and of the formation of fairy tales a
those in accordance with which the dreams are f
Ellis (20) interprets to mean "that the wak
itself is capable of acting in a way resembli
sleeping psychic life and of evolving concept
dreams." Civilized man of to-day does not dr
tion from his dreams but primitive man an
Among them the laws of the waking life "are
differentiated from the laws of the sleeping
often find illumination for the problems of o
phenomena of the other" (20). Gross (36)
in which children brought criminal charges wh
ently based on dreams. It is noteworthy that
and reveries center around the time of puberty
directly to literary activity. The celebrated
George Sand developed around the central figu
first seen in a real dream.

The so-called "continued story" shows the p
in the process of mythformation. Leoroyd (51)
these stories may begin early in life, in the f
continue for several years. They are most prom
adolescence and especially in girls and may not b
late in life. The characters are mostly from
often the author himself plays a very prominen
lock Ellis (19) maintains that these stories a

strongly with sexual emotions which are frequently their real motive. This may, however, be so skillfully concealed that it may be difficult to detect it.

All these psychic phenomena are strictly private and intimate experiences which the subjects harbor for themselves. They are strongly emotional and contain a wish realized in them. They form an outlet for the suppressed wishes and emotions which have not been otherwise realized.

The hero-myths or sagas belong to the same class of mental phenomena They are the fulfilment of wishes which for some reason or other could not be fulfilled in any other way. Thus the Oedipus saga is nothing but the fancy formation of an adolescent youth who in his childhood had been estranged from his father, because he separated him from his mother. His wishes developed into a fancy of the death of the father and the marriage of the mother. That the creator of the myth realizes that the whole thing is an outrageous wrong is seen in the later development of the saga. The whole affair is condemned by the hero himself and as punishment blinds himself. The only thing that is put up as an excuse is that in "dreams men often see themselves united to their mothers," but this is put in the mouth of somebody else.

May be there is a genetic significance in this. In ancient time, and in modern times too, it often happened that the father was a strange person, a despot in the family. He ruled over the family as a chief over his tribe and in many cases exercised his power in a not altogether friendly way. This may have aroused an unconscious wish, and perhaps even conscious, to remove him, and to take his position. This often happened. May not this attitude be transmitted and may it not have taken expression in some mental activity such as dreams, day-dreams, and reveries? That the children and primitive man do not consciously realize what death means is pointed out by Abraham (1) and seen in the behavior of every child. To them it means nothing but being away, or not present at the time being. Therefore when it is said that the child wishes his father dead he does not include in this idea the same thing as older people do. But the real cause for the wish is unknown. The child has no idea of the import of his immediate thought. Der kleine Hans often surprised his father by saying: "The thought

occurred to me," "I happened to think of . . . .
he himself had had nothing to do with the thought.
Oedipus saga shows that when he realized the imp
dreamery, a wholly different mental procedure starte

Riklin (67) has called attention to the two diffe
in which the wish structure appears in fairy tale
which have a more or less clear teleological signific
first are those cases in which someone has lost a
friend whom he mourns bitterly and who, after days
and grief, appears to him and asks him not to weep
because his tears and mourning disturb him in his
fanciful belief has become a psychic cure for the livin
it was apparently meant for the dead.

The second and more common form of this kin
structure is the one in which the so-called "Ellenbog
or the slow, stupid, good-for-nothing children who
treated with ridicule and made to do what nobody
to do, come out triumphant over their more favored
The fulfilment of a wish is so plain here that it is
to mistake it. It is the same psychic activity as
the hero-myths in general. The poor boy or girl b
son or daughter of a rich and beautiful king in a ve
stantial way and afterwards marries into a rich f
becomes very famous to the great dismay of his
pressors. That difficulties encounter them in their
realize their wish in their fancy makes the whole situ
romantic and fascinating and shows that mind does
run the straight and easy path to a desired goal
indulges in the most trying and perplexing circumst
an ease and unconcern that is almost appalling.

But in many cases the troubles which the hero
contend with start at birth and sometimes even b
children they have been rejected and exposed but r
brought up by brutes or low people. We meet the
in the maxim "Nemo propheta in patria," which ha
meaning than that a man whose parents, brothers, sist
etc., are well known, must renounce these at least
if he wishes to be recognized as great. This brea
of the children from the parents is an evolutionar
but to be sure a painful experience.

In the development of the child there is a time when the parents are everything for him. His most intense wish is to become like them. But he soon learns to know other people who appear to him greater. Small events in his life call forth unsatisfactory feelings. The glory of other people and the disregard shown by his own parents give rise to the wish of belonging to them and perhaps he goes so far as to imagine himself child of other people. This idea comes out strongly in the psycho-nuerotics who have exaggerated the infantile fancies in a high degree from lack of any controlling elements. But the fictitious father of the hero has often the most pronounced characteristics of the real father and is therefore not a substitution but a transference for the purpose of fulfilling the wish. The whole thing is an expression of the longing for those happy days when the father was the noblest man and the mother the most lovely woman on earth.

The hero of the saga echoes in this way the egoistic feelings of the child, which are counteracted by other interests and so suppressed,

## V. Summary

Myth is the expression of primitive man's thoughts and feelings concerning himself and the external world and the gods. It has to be sure some connection with the changes of language, but it is more intimately bound up with the human psyche which tends to express itself in some way peculiarly its own. This accounts for the fact that the mythologizing idea has never left man but still lingers and finds expression in the folk-poetry and folk-tales of different people. The myth and poetry are very closely connected, and the more poetry resembles myth the more universal it becomes and loses its individual character.

Whether man has developed slowly, by sudden partial leaps, or by a sudden leap in toto, or whether he has originated from one pair in one place only or from several, does not make so much difference after all, for in either case the evolutional laws must have been the same that brought about the development which resulted in the being we now call man. But if the leap was in toto and too sudden the effect might have been detrimental because of the sudden separation from the preceding stage into the new environment which he was not accustomed to.

Mind has developed along similar lines according to simila laws everywhere which makes mind one and makes it possibl for one man to understand another. They both have a huma mind. In this development we find the reason for the similarit of so many myths which could not have been borrowed by on people from another. Moreover, the theory of borrowing doe not explain anything and is in reality very superficial.

The myths may be divided into two large groups, Natur myths and Hero myths or Culture myths. The nature myth may again be divided into such that have sprung up aroun natural objects and such that have sprung up around natura phenomena. There is hardly any object or any phenomeno which has not at some time or other been subject for a myth All groups of natural objects and all kinds of natural phe nomena have attracted primitive man's attention and cause him to wonder and speculate. The tendency that has bee current to exalt one object at the expense of another must b rejected. The moon for instance has exerted a greater influ ence upon man than the sun, although the sun has been regarde as superior. Superior it may be but not in its effect upo man's behavior. The reason for this may be found in th natural phenomenon itself as well as in the environment an mental attitude of man. At night man could look at and medi tate upon the moon. He had leisure to do so, and the sur roundings were more favorable for an emotional impression.

If any object has played a greater rôle in man's life tha the other, it is the tree. World-trees are found all over th world, sacred trees are common, and trees and groves actuall worshipped, found all over the world. A great tree-lore ha sprung up around these which still exerts a profound influence The reason for this has been sought in the intimate relation ship which is thought to have existed between man and th tree. From the tree man is supposed to have gathered hi food, in the tree he is supposed to have lived, and to the tre he is supposed to have fled in times of danger. The theory of his arboreal life has, however, lately been disputed. Be tha as it may, one thing is sure, man and the tree have been ver closely connected.

Man projected himself into the objects and phenomena; h personified them or perhaps better he elementarized himself

He ascribed the same attributes and qualities which he possessed to the world around him. He used himself as a measure and explanation of all things. His gods were also formed in his own image because he was the object of his conceptions. They were the natural outgrowth of his inability to cope with a given situation, and of his feeling of dependency developed during his long infancy. Where man considered himself immortal his gods were also immortal. They shared the common fate of man. Among some people they were maintained in vigor and youth by a special prerogative which was denied man. In the other world gods and men are again going to live together in peace and harmony pursuing their various occupations. In a word, the gods were men more and more magnified, with human desires and human wants

The hero myths are also the expression of the human psyche but in a different way from the nature myths In them the emotions on the one hand and the customs and traditions on the other play the dominant part. The underlying factor is the question of seeking pleasure and avoiding pain. The soul is a great center of psychic force which endeavors to express itself according to its own nature. Most primordial are the nutritive and sexual emotions which therefore play the greater rôle. Of these the sexual emotion is the strongest and lies at the bottom of shame, modesty, and morality. Even the child is not free from this emotion and his first sexual object is the parent of the opposite sex, according to Freud. When the emotions want to discharge the energy, or when the psyche wants to act out its impulses, it finds that society has established a certain standard according to which they are to be acted out. But this standard has not taken all the possibility into consideration and many of the emotional impulses are not provided for. They can not be provided for either, for the individual must be subordinate to the society in which he lives. As a result the emotional impulses find themselves at variance with the standards of society and must either disregard the custom and traditions and act them out or else suppress them. If they are suppressed, they can nevertheless not be gotten rid of, because they are dynamic. The energy can not be lost. Below the threshold of consciousness, in what Freud calls the subconscious. these emotional impulses are still active and influence the conscious life indirectly. They are waiting for an opportunity to express themselves. But since the organism has learned to seek pleasure and avoid pain, and since they were suppressed in the first place because they caused more pain than pleasure, they can not enter consciousness or express themselves in their real garb. Therefore they must find some way in which they can escape the censor which the customs and traditions have built up. This they find in transferring their energy to other objects which thus symbolize them but have not their painful character. The suppressed emotions and wishes find the easiest expression when the conscious life is lowered as in dreams, day-dreams, and reveries. The hero myths are the fancy-realisation of the suppressed emotions and wishes which could not be fulfilled in any other way. They are the dreams of the childhood of the race in which the individuals imagined themselves in the positions described in the sagas.

But not only the sagas are the expressions of these suppressed wishes and emotional impulses. Much of what is worth while in arts, literature, and religion, is an expression of the same psychic energy which was once forbidden. Traces of them are found everywhere in painting, scultpure, drama, and poetry. The energy of these suppressed emotions and wishes thus finds expression sublimated, on a higher plane, and colors the life of every being. Emotional individuals are affected more than other, but their imagination is also more creative and full of ideas.

## Bibliography


1. Abraham, Karl. Traum und Mythos, Eine Studie zur Völkerpsychologie. Deuticke, Leipzig und Wien, 1909. 73 p.
2. ———. Giovanni Segantini. Deuticke, Leipzig und Wien, 1911, 63 p.
3. Aschaffenburg, G. Experimentelle Studien über Association. Kraepelin Psych. Arb. Vol. I, 1899, pp. 209-300, Vol. II, 1900, pp. 1-84, Vol. III, 1904, pp. 235-375.
4. Baldwin, J. M. Mental Development in the Child and the Races. Macmillan, New York, 1906, 477 p.
5. Bastian, A. Zur Naturwissenschaftlichen Behandlungsweise der Psycologie durch und für die Völkerkunde. Weidman, Berlin, 1883, XXVIII-230 p.
6. Baring-Gould, S. Curious Myths of the Middle Ages. Rivington, London, 1868, 660 p.
7. Bell, Sanford. A Preliminary Study of the Emotion of Love between the Sexes. *Am. J. of Psych.*. Vol. XIII, 1902, pp. 325-354.

8. BOAS, FRANZ. Psychological Problems in Anthropology. *Am. J. of Psych.*, *Vol.* XXI, 1910, pp. 371-384.
9. ———. Mind of Primitive Man. Macmillan, New York, 1911, 294 p.
10. BRINTON, D. G. Religions of Primitive Peoples. Putnam, New York, 1898, 264 p
11 ———. The Myths of the New World, A Treatise on the Symbolism and Mythology of the Red Race of America. McKay, Philadelphia, 1896, 360 p.
12. ———. American Hero Myths. A Study in the Native Religions of the Western Continent. Watts, Philadelphia, 1882, 239 p.
13. CHASE, H. W. Psychoanalysis and the Unconscious. *Ped. Sem.*, Vol. XVII, 1911, pp 281-327.
14, COX, SIR G. W. The Mythology of the Aryan Nations. Paul, Trench & Co, London, 1887, XXVIII-594 p.
15. CRAWLEY, A. E. Sexual Taboo. A Study in the Relations of the Sexes. *Jour. Anthrop. Inst.*, Vol. XXIV, 1895, pp. 430-446.
16. DARMESTETER, J. The Zend Avesta. Clarendon Press, Oxford, 1883, Part II, 384 p.
17. DASENT, SIR G. W. Popular Tales from the Norse. Douglas, Edinburgh, 1903, CLXXVII-443.
18. DUBOIS, ABBE J. A. Hindu Manners, Customs and Ceremonies. Clarendon Press, Oxford, 1906, 741 p.
19. ELLIS, HAVELOCK. Studies in the Psychology of Sex. Davis & Co, Philadelphia, 1900, Vol. II, 313 p.
20. ———. The World of Dreams. Houghton Mifflin, Boston, 1911, 288 p
21. EHRENREICH, P. Die Allgemeine Mythologie und ihre ethnologischen Grundlagen. Hinrich, Leipzig, 1910, 288 p.
22. FERENCZI, S. Introjektion und Übertragung. Deuticke, Leipzig und Wien, 1910, 38 p.
23. FISKE, JOHN. Myths and Myth-makers. Houghton Mifflin, Boston, 1888, 251 p.
24. FORLONG, J. G. R. Rivers of Life or Sources of Streams of Faiths of Man in all Lands. Quaritch, London, 1883, 2 vols
25. FRAZER, J. G. The Magic Art. The Golden Bough, Vol. II. Macmillan, New York, 1911, 417 p.
26. GENNEP, A. VAN. La Formation des Legendes Flammarion, Paris, 1910, 326 p.
27. ———. Les Rites de Passage. Flammarion, Paris, 1909, 288 p.
28. FREUD, S. Die Traumdeutung Deuticke, Leipzig und Wien, 1909, 382 p.
29. ———. Three Contributions to the Sexual Theory. Jour. of Nervous and Mental Disease Publ. Co., New York, 1910, 91 p.
30. ———. Selected Papers on Hysteria and other Psychoneuroses. Jour. of Nervous and Mental Disease Publ. Co., New York, 1909, 200 p
31. ———. Sammlung kleiner Schriften zur Neurosenlehre. Deuticke, Leipzig und Wien, 1909, Vol. II, 206 p.
32. ———. Analyse der Phobie eines Fünfjährigen Knaben *Jahrb für* [illegible]

33. ———. Der Wahn und die Träume in Jensen's Gradiva. Deuticke, Leipzig und Wien, 1907, 81 p.

34. ———. Eine Kindheitserinnerung des Leonardo da Vinci. Deuticke, Leipzig und Wien, 1910, 71 p.

35. GRAF, MAX. Richard Wagner im "Fliegenden Holländer." Deuticke, Leipzig und Wien, 1911, 46 p.

36. GROSS, HANS. Kriminalpsychologie. Vogel, Leipzig, 1905, 701 p.

37. HALL, G. STANLEY. Adolescence, its Psychology and its Relation to Physiology, Anthropology, Sociology, Sex, Crime, Religion and Education. Appleton, New York, 1904, 2 vols.

38. ———. A Study of Fear. *Am. J. of Psych.*, Vol. VIII, 1897, pp. 147-249.

39. ———. Professor Edward Zeller. *Am. J. of Psych.*, Vol. IV, 1891, pp. 156-175.

40. HALL, G. STANLEY AND ALLIN, A. The Psychology of Tickling, Laughter and the Comic. *Am. J. of Psych.*, Vol. IX, 1897, pp. 1-41.

41. HARLEY, T. Moon Lore. Sonnenschein, London, 1885, 296 p.

42. HESIOD, ——. Les Travaux et les Jours. Traduit par M. Patin. Granier, Paris, 1882, 280 p.

43. HEWITT, J. N. B. Iroquoian Cosmology. *Bul. of Am. Ethn.*, 1899-1900, pp. 133-339.

44. JEVONS, F. B. The Idea of God in the early Religions. Cambridge, University Press, 1910, 170 p.

45. JEWELL, J. R. The Psychology of Dreams. *Am. J. of Psych.*, Vol. XVI, 1905, pp. 1-34.

46. JUNG, C. & RIKLIN, F. Experimentelle Untersuchungen ueber Assoziation Gesunder. Diag. Assoziationsstudien, Beilag I, Barth, Leipzig, 1906, pp. 7-145.

47. JONES, ERNEST. The Oedipus-Complex as an Explanation of Hamlet's Mystery: A Study in Motive. *Am. J. of Psych.*, Vol. XXI, 1910, pp. 72-113.

48. KLAATSCH, H. Die Todes-Psychologie der Uraustralier in ihrer Volks- und religionsgeschichtlichen Bedeutung. Mitt. d. Schlesischen Ges. f. Volkskunde, Vol. 13-14, 1911-1912, pp. 401-439. Reviewed in *Jour. of Religious Psychology*, Vol. V, 1912, pp. 250-252.

49. KUHN, E. Die Herabkunft des Feuers und des Göttertranks. Bertelsmann, Gutersloh, 1886, 240 p.

50. LANG, A. Custom and Myth. Longmans, Green, London, 1883, 312 p.

51. LEOROYD, MABEL W. The "Continued Story." *Am. J. of Psych.*, Vol. VII, 1895, pp. 86-90.

52. MAHAFFY, J. P. Prolegomena to Ancient History: The Interpretation of Legends and Inscriptions; A Survey of the Old Egyptian Literature. Macmillan, London, 1871, 438 p.

53. MUCH, M. Die Heimat der Indo-Germanen. Costenoble, Jena und Berlin, 1904, 421 p.

54. MÜLLER, MAX. Lectures on Science of Language. Longmans, Green, London, 1866, 2 vols.

55. Newell, W. W Ritual Regarded as the Dramatization of Myth. Memoirs Inter. Cong. of Anthr., 1893, Chicago, 1894, pp. 237-245.

56. Nietzsche, F. Zur Genealogie der Moral. Nietzsche's Werke, Vol. VII, Abt. 1, pp. 287-484, Naumann, Leipzig, 1903.

57. Perez, B. L' Enfant de Trois à Sept Ans. Alcan, Paris, 1888, 307 p.

58. Peters, W. Gefühl und Erinnerung Kraepelin Psych. Arb., Vol. VI, 1911, pp. 197-260.

59. Petrie, W. M. F. The Revolutions of Civilization. Harper & Brothers, New York, 1911, 135 p.

60 Pfister, O. Die Frömmigkeit des Grafen Ludwig von Zinzendorf. Deuticke, Leipzig und Wien, 1910, 122 p.

61. Prince, Morton. The Unconscious. *Jour. of Ab. Psych.*, Vol. III, 1908-9, pp 261-297, pp. 335-353, pp 391-426.

62. Quantz, J. O. Dendro-Psychosis. *Am. J. of Psych.*, Vol. IX, 1898, pp. 448-509.

63. Rank, O Der Mythus von der Geburt des Helden. Deuticke, Leipzig und Wien, 1909, 93 p.

64. ———. Die Lohengrin Sage. Deuticke, Leipzig und Wien, 1911, 181 p.

65. Ribot, T. Psychology of the Emotions. Scribner, New York, 1897, 455 p.

66. Richard, E. The Scandinavian Theory of Indo-European Origins. Boas Anniversary Volume Stechert, New York, 1906, pp. 373-386.

67. Riklin, E. Wunscherfüllung und Symbolik in Märchen. Deuticke, Leipzig und Wien, 1908, 96 p.

67a. Ruskin, J. Queen of the Air. *Ruskin's Works*, Vol. 21, pp. 235-358 Colonial Press, Boston and New York.

68. Rydberg, V. Fädernas Gudasaga Bonnier, Stockholm, 1898, 639 p.

69. Sayce, A H. Ancient Babylonians Hibbert Lectures 1887. William & Norgate, London, 1898, 558 p

70. Schidlof, B. Das Sexualleben der Australier. G. m. b. H., Leipzig, 1908, 314 p.

71. Sergi, G. Les Emotions. Octave Doin, Paris, 1901, 460 p.

72. Smith, R. W. Religion of the Semite. Appleton, New York, 1889, 488 p.

73. Spencer, B. & Gillen, F. J. Native Tribes of Central Australia. Macmillan, New York, 1899, 671 p.

74. Spencer, H. The Principles of Sociology. Appleton, New York (3 vols.), Vol. III, 645 p.

75. Storfer, A. J. Zur Sonderstellung des Vatermordes. Deuticke, Leipzig und Wien, 1911, 34 p.

76 Sutherland, A. The Origin and Growth of the Moral Instinct. Longmans, Green, New York, 2 vols.

77. Tacitus, C Annales, XIII, 55.

78. Taylor, I. The Origin of the Aryans. Scott, London, 1892, 339 p.

79. Tylor, E. B. Primitive Culture. Holt, New York, 1888, 2 vols.

80. Upanishads, ——. 2 vols. Sacred Books of the East. Vols I. and II. Clarendon Press, Oxford, 1879, 1884.

81. Vignoli, T. Myth and Science. Appleton, New York, 1882, 330 p.

82. Virgil, M. P. Aeneid (VIII, 314-5). Trans. by T. C. Williams. Houghton Mifflin, Boston, 1908, 503 p.

83. Voigtländer, Else. Ueber die Bedeutung Freuds für die Psychologie. Münchener Philosophische Abhandlungen. Lipps Festschrift, pp. 294-316. Barth, Leipzig, 1911, 316 p.

84. Wachter, W. Bestia Sum. Eine Kapitel über die Kehrseite des Menschtums. Felber, Berlin, 1908, 261 p.

85. Waitz, Th. Introduction to Anthropology. Longmans, Green, London, 1863, 404 p.

86. Westermarck, E. The Origin and Development of the Moral Ideas. Macmillan, London & New York, 1906, 2 vols.

87. ———. The History of Human Marriage. Macmillan, London & New York, 1901, 644 p.

88. Wundt, W. Völkerpsychologie. Engelmann, Leipzig, 5 vols. (vol. 2, Bd. 1).

89. Zeller, E. Über Ursprung und Wesen der Religion. In Vorträge und Abhandlungen, Vol. II, pp. 1-92. Fues, Leipzig, 1877.

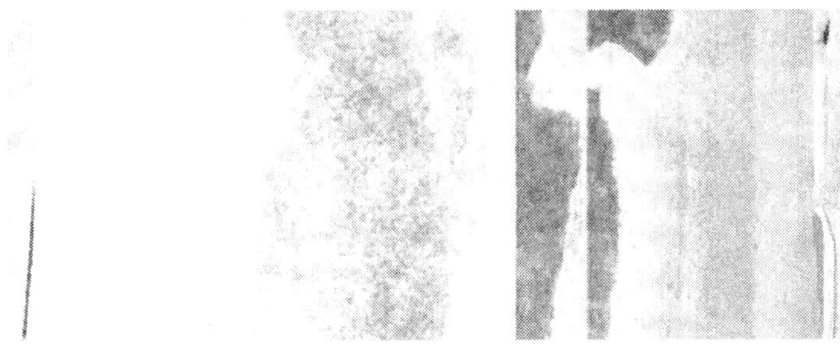

www.ingramcontent.com/pod-product-compliance
Ingram Content Group UK Ltd.
Pitfield, Milton Keynes, MK11 3LW, UK
UKHW020708110526
12378UKWH00045B/1136